DIEU ET MON DROIT

THE QUEEN
E II R

THE LIFE AND TIMES OF ELIZABETH II

CATHERINE RYAN

CHARTWELL
BOOKS

HER MAJESTY
QUEEN ELIZABETH II

Elizabeth II (born 1926) has been Queen of the United Kingdom, Canada, Australia, and New Zealand since February 6, 1952. She has reigned longer than any other British monarch and is the longest-reigning female head of state in world history.

CONTENTS

INTRODUCTION

Queen Elizabeth II has reigned longer than any British monarch in history and during that time has endured the many ups and downs that a long life will bring. She was the jewel in the crown during and after the Second World War in difficult times when the world faced a precarious future. She has since served as a role model for generations of men and women who continue to be in awe of her commitment to service, sacrifice, and the Commonwealth of nations over which she rules.

When she came into the world in April 1926, however, sovereignty over thirty-two countries and rule over two billion subjects appeared to be a highly unlikely prospect for her. Rather, it seemed as if she was destined to live a quiet life far from the spotlight, perhaps breeding the horses she loves so much or walking her corgi dogs on a country estate. Fate had other ideas though, and the abdication of her uncle, Edward VIII, in 1936 turned her family's world upside-down. When her father was crowned King George VI, Elizabeth was thrust into the eye of the storm as the future queen.

A shy and reserved child, she grew into a wise and insightful monarch who has dealt ably with thirteen prime ministers and thirteen US presidents during her long reign. She has not always seen eye to eye with their policies but has always succeeded in maintaining her neutrality as a constitutional monarch, eschewing the expression of an opinion but always *au fait* with reality.

Her attention is always focused on the survival of the institution of monarchy. In a rapidly changing world the deference once shown to the royal family has become a thing of the past and the media feels free to delve into private lives and create scandalous stories in any way they see fit. This has caused undoubted problems for Her Majesty and her family over the last few decades and it has taken them a long time to adjust to the complexities of celebrity in the modern age. But lessons have been learned and mistakes admitted and her family finds itself in good shape as the twenty-first century progresses.

Princess Elizabeth (later Queen Elizabeth II) and the Duke of Edinburgh in 1950.

It was not always thus, and the Queen has found herself in hot water several times, most notably during the marriage of Prince Charles and Princess Diana when her standing and that of her family was probably at its lowest ebb. It may have been partly the fault of Elizabeth's upbringing that produced the crisis following Diana's death in a Paris car crash. The insistence that the royals should never show emotion in public, that a stiff upper lip was the order of the day. Thus, during that extraordinary week in 1997, the Queen seemed bewildered by the outpouring of grief for her dead daughter-in-law. The people wanted her to show some emotion in the face of such grief, even if it was only manifested in the lowering of a flag over Buckingham Palace.

The crisis was weathered eventually and there has been a recent resurgence of love for the Queen. The wedding of Prince William and Catherine Middleton in 2011 and the Queen's Diamond Jubilee in 2012 saw a renewal of respect for the royal family. The birth of a new generation in the form of William's children, Prince George and Princess Charlotte, has created new hope for the future of the monarchy, to take it into the next century.

It is unlikely that we will ever see a monarch reign so long or so effectively again, holding together a disparate group of nations, each with its own aspirations, customs, and traditions. It is estimated that the Queen has traveled more than a million miles—the equivalent of traveling round the world forty-two times—and only recently did she decide to give up the long haul aspect of her travels. At 91 years of age, it is probably about time!

One thing is certain however. As long as there is a breath in her body, she will persevere with the solemn commitment she made at her coronation while still a young woman, to dedicate her life to her country, her Commonwealth, and her loyal subjects.

The Queen meets well-wishers in Glasgow during a visit to Scotland as part of her Diamond Jubilee Tour, 2012.

PART ONE

THE JEWEL
IN THE CROWN

I declare before you all that my whole life whether it be long or short shall be devoted to your service and the service of our great imperial family to which we all belong.

Princess Elizabeth on her 21st birthday, 1947

CHAPTER 1

A BEACON OF HOPE

In April 1926, Hindus and Muslims were rioting in Calcutta; Violet Gibson (1876 – 1956), the Irish daughter of Lord Ashbourne, tried to assassinate the Italian leader Benito Mussolini (1883 – 1945) in Rome; the army of the Manchurian warlord Zhang Zuolin (1875 – 1928) entered Beijing in China; Reza Shah Pahlavi (1878 – 1944) was crowned Shah of Iran.

In Britain, a million British coal miners rejected a final offer from the mine owners of a 13 percent pay cut and an increase in their working day from seven to eight hours. The prospect of a miners' strike was concerning to the government, the leader of the miners, A.J. Cook (1883 – 1931) doggedly proclaiming in a speech, "Not a penny off the pay, not a minute on the day."

Amid the troubles of the world, at 2:40 a.m. on April 21, at number 17 Bruton Street in London's exclusive Mayfair district, a baby was born. Named Elizabeth Alexandra Mary, she was the daughter of the Duke (1895 – 1952) and Duchess of York (1900 – 2002). The Duke of York was Prince Albert Frederick Arthur George, brother to the heir to the British Crown, Prince Edward Albert Christian George Andrew Patrick David (1894 – 1972), the Prince of Wales. The baby's mother, the 25-year-old Duchess of York was the former Lady Elizabeth Angela Marguerite Bowes-Lyon.

The delivery of the baby was not without its complications. A statement issued by the Duchess's physicians revealed that "Previous to the confinement a consultation took place ... and a certain line of treatment was successfully

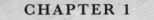

Family group photograph taken after the christening of Princess Elizabeth of York on May 29, 1926. Front row from left to right: Lady Elphinstone (née Lady Mary Bowes-Lyon); Queen Mary; The Duchess of York, holding the infant Princess Elizabeth; The Countess of Strathmore; Princess Mary, Viscountess Lascelles. Back row from left to right: The Duke of Connaught; King George V; The Duke of York; The Earl of Strathmore.

adopted." In other words, the child was delivered by Caesarean section, a procedure not without risks back then. It was clear, given such risks, that the Duke and Duchess would not be having a large family.

This could have been very bad news had Prince Albert been next in line for the throne of the United Kingdom as it would reduce the chance of a male heir. But he was behind his brother David in the line of succession and it appeared highly unlikely that Albert or any member of his immediate family would ever wear the crown. Nonetheless, the new royal baby was third in line behind the Prince of Wales and her father, and a beacon of hope in a world of hurt.

WELCOME TO THE WORLD

There was great excitement at the news of a royal birth. The newspapers led on it and a crowd gathered outside the Bruton Street house, cheering the royal visitors, the first of whom were the baby's grandparents, King George V (1865 – 1936) and Queen Mary (1867 – 1953). Her Majesty fondly described the new arrival as "a little darling with lovely complexion and pretty fair hair." The Duke of York was naturally delighted, if perhaps a little anxious that he and his wife had not provided a male heir. He wrote to his mother:

We always wanted a child to make our happiness complete. I do hope that you and Papa are as delighted as we are, to have a granddaughter, or would you sooner have another grandson? I know Elizabeth wanted a daughter.

Soon, however, other matters were occupying the thoughts of the nation. The situation with the miners remained unresolved and the General Council of the Trades Union Congress (TUC) called a General Strike of railwaymen, transport workers, printers, dockers, ironworkers, and steelworkers. Around 1.7 million workers withdrew their labor. The strike created chaos across the country from May 3 until 13.

The newly-born Princess Elizabeth with her father and mother, the Duke and Duchess of York, 1926.

The Bowes-Lyon Family

The Bowes-Lyon family descended from the County Durham landowner and politician, George Bowes (1701 – 60) of Gibside and Streatlam Castle, through John Bowes, 9th Earl of Strathmore and Kinghorne (1737 – 76) who was chief of the Clan Lyon. Born John Lyon, the Earl was famous for his appearance and not for nothing was he known as "the beautiful Lord Strathmore."

In 1767, the Earl married an heiress, Mary Eleanor Bowes, assuming her surname as stipulated in her father's will, a change that required an Act of Parliament, although it was not an unusual occurrence among the landed classes at this time.

Claude Bowes-Lyon, the 14th and 1st Earl of Strathmore and Kinghorne (1855 – 1944) was born in Lowndes Square, London. He was educated at Eton College and served for 6 years as an officer in the 2nd Life Guards in 1876. He married Cecilia Cavendish-Bentinck in 1881 and they had ten children. Claude inherited his father's title of Earl of Strathmore and Kinghorne in 1904, whereupon Cecilia became Countess of Strathmore and Kinghorne.

Upon succeeding his father to the Earldom, Claude inherited estates in Scotland and England, including Glamis Castle, St. Paul's Walden Bury, and Woolmers Park, near Hertford. His contemporaries described him as an unpretentious man who was often seen in "an old macintosh tied with a piece of twine." Visitors frequently mistook him for one of the estate gardeners.

In 1923, the Bowes-Lyon's youngest daughter, Elizabeth, married King George V's second son, Prince Albert, the Duke of York, and became the Duchess of York.

Claude and Cecilia Bowes-Lyon, the Earl and Countess of Strathmore, parents of the Duchess of York.

The Duke and Duchess of York

Elizabeth Bowes-Lyon and her siblings were friends of the children of George V from an early age. By the time she was 18, Elizabeth had become a strikingly attractive woman who drew the attention of many potential suitors among whom was Prince Albert.

Prince Albert (known as Bertie) was a shy, insecure man, partly as a result of his stammer but was soon a regular visitor to Glamis Castle. Queen Mary spotted the attraction early in the relationship, saying to Lady Airlie: "I have discovered that [Bertie] is very much attracted to Lady Elizabeth Bowes-Lyon. He's always talking about her. She seems a charming girl but I don't know her very well." Lady Airlie concurred: "I have known her all her life and could say nothing but good about her."

Bertie first proposed to Elizabeth in the spring of 1921, but she rejected his proposal. He was undaunted and had the support of his mother who believed Elizabeth to be "the one girl who could make Bertie happy." He proposed again in February 1922 when Elizabeth was a bridesmaid at the wedding of his sister, Princess Mary (1897 – 1965) to Viscount Lascelles (1882 – 1947), but once again she spurned him.

In January 1923, he tried again. He was visiting her at the Bowes-Lyon Hertfordshire home of St. Paul's Walden Bury and, skipping church, the two went for a morning walk in the woods. He proposed and this time she said yes. Bertie despatched a telegram to his parents with the agreed message: "All right. Bertie."

On April 26, 1923, the couple were married in Westminster Abbey, Elizabeth laying her bouquet on the Tomb of the Unknown Warrior on her way into the abbey in memory of her brother Fergus (1889 – 1915) who had died at the age of 26 in the First World War. It is a tradition that has carried on for royal brides although it is now done after the ceremony. The couple spent their honeymoon at Polesdon Lacey, a manor house in Surrey owned by the well-known society figure and hostess Margaret Greville (1863 – 1942).

Albert and Elizabeth, the Duke and Duchess of York on their wedding day.

Workers took to the streets to demonstrate as the government appealed for volunteers to help maintain essential services. The Emergency Powers Act 1920 was used in order to maintain essential supplies. Debates in the House of Commons were closely followed and the Duke of York was there every day to watch them. Austerity measures were introduced. At Buckingham Palace, the customary red uniforms of the sentries were changed to khaki and many of the royal household were employed as special constables.

Interest in the royal baby persisted, however, and even as late as May 14, when the Countess of Airlie (1866 – 1956), lady-in-waiting to Queen Mary, arrived in Bruton Street bearing a bottle of "Jordan water" from the Holy Land that was to be used in the baby's christening, crowds still thronged the pavements.

SETTING A SENSIBLE STYLE

Princess Elizabeth, dressed in a robe several feet long, cried a great deal during her christening at Buckingham Palace, to the extent that after the service her old-fashioned nurse plied her with dill water from a bottle. This was to the great surprise of some of "the modern young mothers present," which is how Lady Airlie described the friends of the Duchess who were in attendance.

With the christening out of the way, the media began to debate how the Princess should be brought up. Should she have a modern upbringing, or should the Duke and Duchess fall back on tradition? The consensus opted for a "sensible" upbringing with the emphasis firmly on orderliness, routine and a disdain for whatever was fashionable in the world of child-rearing.

There should be none of the type of luxury her position might have brought. Her clothes, for instance, should be handmade of the finest materials and the Queen, Lady Strathmore (the Duchess's mother) and the Duchess were praised for having personally stitched the child's layette along with the help of the inmates of charitable institutions.

In fact, the Duchess was a believer in modern methods and in modern dress, favoring shorter skirts for her daughter. She also preferred cotton to wool. The clothes she selected for her daughter would not be showy in any way, and frilliness was more about femininity than adornment, to her mind. Simplicity was her preference and, as a rule, while Princess Elizabeth was a baby and a toddler she would be seen dressed in white.

As she got older, the Duchess ensured that her clothes were simple. This simple, sensible style of dress represented an outward manifestation of an uncomplicated life and upbringing. In fact, even in adolescence, the Princess appeared to be not particularly bothered about what she wore.

A HOUSE IN PICCADILLY

At Bruton Street, Princess Elizabeth had a room that was, according to Lady Strathmore, "typically English," but soon the entire household was uprooted and moved to a new address at 145 Piccadilly—a white terraced building close to Hyde Park Corner.

It was a large property with twenty-five bedrooms and servants' quarters, the Duke and Duchess maintaining a full retinue while they lived there. Among their many staff were a steward, a housekeeper, the Duchess's maid, a valet for the Duke, two footmen, three further maids, a cook, and two kitchen maids. There was also a nurse, a nursery-maid, a boy, and a night-watchman.

The house was decorated in a style favored by the Duchess with large oil paintings, often featuring horses, in heavy gilt frames. Massive elephant tusks—mementos, no doubt, of a big game hunt—stood in the dim entrance hall. At the rear there was a large garden that the surrounding houses shared. This later provided the Princess with a play area, but soon the public and the press became aware that the little girl skipping or running that they could see through the railings was no ordinary child.

Elizabeth's quarters were located at the top of the house. There she enjoyed a day nursery, a night nursery, and a bathroom, with a landing whose large windows overlooked the park. It was all presided over by the Yorks' nanny, Clara Knight (1879 – 1946) whom the children came to know as "Allah." She had looked after the Duchess and her brother when they were young and she was a formidable presence in the household, a person who did not appreciate modern methods of child-rearing.

Allah was helped by the Scottish nursemaid, Bobo MacDonald (1904 – 93) who was described by another member of staff as "small, very smart, and rather peremptory." Bobo remained with the Queen until 1993. As the Yorks assumed a more serious royal role, such people became increasingly important in the life of the young Princess.

THE DUKE AND DUCHESS GO TRAVELING

From birth, Princess Elizabeth spent a great deal of time in Scotland, either staying with her Strathmore-Bowes-Lyons grandparents in the ancient nursery wing at their ancestral seat, Glamis Castle in Angus, or with her royal grandparents at Balmoral Castle in Royal Deeside, Aberdeenshire. Her first summer was spent at Glamis Castle but at the end of August she was left with the Countess of Strathmore while her parents set off on a series of visits to family and friends. It was what people of their class did.

Soon, however, the Princess was to face an even longer separation from her parents. The Duke had agreed to open the Australian Commonwealth Parliament in Canberra, Australia. The Duchess would of course be traveling with him, but their daughter would stay at home. After Christmas she was deposited at the Strathmores' home, St. Paul's Walden Bury in Hertfordshire. The Yorks sailed out of Portsmouth on the battle cruiser, HMS *Renown*, in early January 1927, the Duchess expressing her regret at leaving her 8-month-old baby in a letter to Queen Mary:

> [I] felt very much leaving on Thursday, and the baby was so sweet playing with the buttons on Bertie's uniform that it quite broke me up.

Nonetheless, it was not unusual for royals to depart on a trip leaving their children behind. George V had done it while he and his wife made visits to far-flung corners of the British Empire.

Princess Elizabeth as a baby in 1927, with nanny Clara Knight.

BUCKINGHAM PALACE

The balcony at Buckingham Palace represents a focal point for national celebration, a war won, a marriage entered, or a birthday celebrated. It has been the scene of many iconic moments in British history. In fact, the balcony is just a small part of the remodeling of what can be regarded as London's ceremonial center in the late nineteenth and early twentieth centuries. It was a period of rampant imperial ambition

and this was expressed ever more grandiosely across the great cities of Europe and the world. The cities of Berlin, Mexico City, Oslo, Paris, St. Petersburg, Vienna, and Washington DC already enjoyed ceremonial routes.

A plan was created for a triumphal ceremonial route in the heart of London by widening the Mall, the thoroughfare that leads from Trafalgar Square to Buckingham Palace, constructing

Admiralty Arch which was completed in 1912, building the Victoria Memorial (not completed until 1924) and redesigning the front of the palace itself, incorporating the large balcony that is seen today. There had been a veranda there before and the royal family had appeared on it since the Great Exhibition of 1851, but the new version is far grander than the old one and is the focal point of the East Front of Buckingham Palace, its main entrance.

On important occasions, people assemble in front of the gates and await the emergence of the royals. Thus, on August 4, 1914, George V was summoned by people cheering three times onto the balcony to signify his approval of the nation entering World War I with Germany. For his part, he took the cheers of the people as support for the war. The balcony probably achieved popularity after the Armistice was signed in November 1918 and the new medium of film was able to show the spectacle to many millions who lived far from the nation's capital.

The first royal newlyweds to appear on the balcony were Princess Mary and her husband, the daughter of George V, and it was a tradition that carried on through to the weddings of Prince Charles and Lady Diana Spencer, and Prince William and Catherine Middleton. Coronations, state events, and celebrations all justify a royal appearance on the iconic balcony, creating a symbolic connection between the British people and the crown.

A parade of the Household Cavalry Mounted Regiment as part of the Trooping the Color ceremony outside Buckingham Palace. Originally built in 1703, Buckingham Palace is the London home of the Queen, and is often at the center of state occasions. The famous balcony can be seen at the front, draped in red and gold.

THE DUKE OF YORK'S SPEECH

THE AUSTRALIAN TOUR

The Duke of York had stammered since the age of 7 and as a child was extremely shy, not a character trait that suited the role he had been given in life. So far, he had not been required to do very much but he was wary of occasions where he might be required to speak publicly.

In fact, there were some advantages to his speech problems. As he did not often appear in public, there was less interest in him than there might have been, and he and his family were largely untroubled by photographers or newsreel cameramen. Marriage had improved his confidence and he had made serious preparations for the visit to Australia, soliciting the help of an Australian speech therapist, Lionel Logue (1880 – 1953), to reduce his embarrassment when speaking in public.

The Australian tour would be exacting. The Duke and Duchess were traveling via the Panama Canal to Fiji and then on to New Zealand before their ultimate arrival in Sydney. Once in Australia, they were to undertake visits to a number of Australian cities, finally arriving in Canberra where the Duke was to deliver his speech.

Not much was really known about the royal couple which meant that the press took a keen interest in their every move and poured over the details of their lives. The public were intrigued by them, especially their daughter back in the mother country. They received letters addressed to the Princess from Australian children and the Duke wrote to his mother: "Wherever we go cheers are given for her as well." It was estimated that around three tonnes of toys were presented as gifts to "Betty" as she became known in the Australian press.

COMING HOME

Back home, however, little had changed and Allah maintained her rigorous discipline, the Princess allowed only to play with one toy at a time. In February 1927, she and the baby were living at Buckingham Palace but in April, when the royal court decamped to Windsor Castle, Allah and the Princess joined them, the baby celebrating her first birthday there, still separated from her parents.

The King and Queen, however, seem to have enjoyed her company and in the afternoons, when she was brought down to them, Queen Mary is reported as always exclaiming: "Here comes the Bambino!" Meanwhile, her progress was being reported to the royal couple in Australia and photographs were sent. She spoke her first word while staying at St. Paul's Walden Bury during the last couple of months of her parents' absence, uttering "Mummy." It was a word she applied to everyone and everything, apparently.

The Duke and Duchess finally returned home in June but it must have been strange. Their daughter had grown and was unlike the baby they had left behind six months previously. But they were laden with gifts for her and the King and Queen and the Strathmores organized a welcome party in Buckingham Palace's Grand Hall. The Duchess was especially delighted to be able to hold her baby in her arms once more.

Lionel Logue

Born in Adelaide in Australia, Lionel George Logue (1880 — 1953) was the grandson of a Dublin-born brewer and his father was an accountant for the firm, Logue's Brewery. He attended Prince Alfred College between 1889 and 1906 and developed an interest in voices. He worked for an elocution teacher as a secretary and assistant teacher from 1902 while also studying music at the Elder Conservatorium in Adelaide. He began to give recitals and received praise for his "clear, powerful voice." Soon, he had launched his own school of elocution but left it to work as an electrician at a gold mine in Kalgoorlie in Western Australia.

He lived in Perth for a while, making a living as an elocution teacher but also acting and taking part in recitals. In 1911, he set off with his wife on a tour of the world, studying public speaking which later led to him developing treatments for Australian First World War veterans who suffered from speech difficulties as a result of shell shock. His methods were novel, involving humor and sympathy.

In 1924, he taught elocution in London schools before opening a practice in Harley Street. Shortly after, the Duke of York asked Logue to help him. The Duke had, of course, had to give speeches but when he spoke at the opening of the British Empire Exhibition at Wembley on October 31, 1925, it was a painful ordeal for both speaker and audience. Recognizing that the Duke's stammer was the result of poor coordination between his larynx and his thoracic diaphragm, Logue prescribed a daily hour of vocal exercises. These helped the Duke to relax and his stammer was greatly reduced. He successfully negotiated his 1927 speech at the opening of the Old Parliament House in Canberra.

Throughout the 1930s and 1940s, Logue continued to work with the Duke, helping him to deliver major speeches and radio broadcasts and to get through his coronation without stammering. The King remained friends with Logue until his death and appointed him a Commander of the Royal Victorian Order. A hugely successful film—*The King's Speech*—was made in 2010 about the Duke's struggle to speak without impediment.

Lionel Logue with his wife, Myrtle Gruenert, in 1906.

King George V

Prince George Frederick Ernest Albert was born in 1865, the second son of the Prince and Princess of Wales, Albert Edward (later King Edward VII, 1841 – 1910) and Princess Alexandra of Denmark (1844 – 1925). Edward VII was the oldest son of Queen Victoria and Prince Albert, and Princess Alexandra was the oldest daughter of King Christian IX of Denmark (1818 – 1906). At the time of his birth, George was third in line to the throne of the United Kingdom, behind his father and his older brother, Prince Albert Victor, Duke of Clarence and Avondale (1864 – 92).

In 1877, he and his brother joined the cadet training ship HMS *Britannia* at Dartmouth in Devon and from 1879 to 1882, they served on HMS *Bacchante*, traveling widely. Albert Victor then went to Trinity College, Cambridge, while George continued with his career in the Royal Navy. His last command was HMS *Melampus* on which he served from 1891 to 1892.

In November 1891, Albert Victor became engaged to Princess Victoria Mary of Teck, known to her family as May. Six weeks later, however, the Prince died of pneumonia. George, who had only recently recovered from typhoid, was now second in line to the throne. During the mourning period, May and George became close and a year after his brother's death, he proposed to her. They were married on July 6, 1893.

Created Duke of York, he never resumed his naval career but instead lived a quiet life. His biographer, Harold Nicholson wrote of him: "He may be all right as a young midshipman and a wise old king, but when he was Duke of York ... he did nothing at all but kill animals and stick in stamps."

George and May had five sons and a daughter and he was a very strict father. He once remarked: "My father was frightened of his mother, I was frightened of my father, and I am damned well going to see to it that my children are frightened of me."

In 1901, Queen Victoria died and George's father acceded to the throne as Edward VII. George inherited the titles of Duke of Cornwall and Duke of Rothesay and became popularly known as the "Duke of Cornwall and York." On November 9, 1901, after a tour of the British Empire, he was created Prince of Wales and Earl of Chester. His father was preparing him for his future role as king by giving him access to state papers, something that Victoria had not been prepared to do for him.

Edward VII died on May 6, 1910, and George became King George V while his wife became Queen Mary, dropping "Victoria" from her title. Their coronation took place on June 22, 1911. That same year the King and Queen traveled to India where they were proclaimed Emperor and Empress of India.

During the First World War, in the face of anti-German sentiment, George issued a royal proclamation, changing his family's name from the German-sounding Saxe-Coburg and Gotha to Windsor. Meanwhile, his cousin, Prince Louis of Battenberg changed his surname to Mountbatten.

Two months after the war ended, George and Mary's youngest son, Prince John (1905 – 19), died at age 13 after a lifetime of poor health. Meanwhile, his relationship with his oldest son and heir to the throne, Edward, deteriorated badly. The King was concerned at the Prince's failure to marry as well as his many affairs with married women.

He said of Edward in 1935: "After I am dead, the boy will ruin himself in twelve months." By this time, he was hoping that his other son George would take the throne. George V died on January 20, 1936, and 326 days later Edward VIII abdicated.

HIS MAJESTY
KING GEORGE V

George V (1865 – 1936) was King of the United Kingdom and the British Dominions, and Emperor of India, from May 6, 1910, until his death in 1936. He was the second son of King Edward VII, and grandson of Queen Victoria.

SWEET SERENITY

The Yorks were glad to be home, but after resting for a few weeks they were off again. The Duke joined the Duchess of Devonshire (1870 – 1960), Mistress of the Robes to the Queen, for the shooting season, while his wife went north to Glamis to visit her parents.

Initially, Elizabeth remained in London but she soon traveled to Glamis to be reunited with her mother and she began to walk. In September, the Duke, Duchess, and Elizabeth were at Balmoral with the King and Queen before returning to London once more.

At this point, Princess Elizabeth had blond curls and blue eyes and already the world was beginning to fabricate a personality for her. Some described her as bright and intelligent as well as generous and pleasantly natured. Another view of her presented a normal, British child. She was sometimes given a somewhat ethereal quality, one writer saying that she had:

> *... the sweetest air of complete serenity about her. While we were talking, her nurse came in to fetch her, and the Duchess threw round her daughter's head ... a filmy veil of gossamer from which she looked down out of her nurse's arms smiling angelically at her mother, like a cherub out of a cloud.*

THE ROGUISH PRINCESS

She was also mischievous however, with one anecdote describing her pelting guests at a Christmas party at Sandringham with crackers. At the age of about 3, she told one guest at Glamis Castle that she had been very naughty. "You can't think how naughty I've been," she said. "Oh *so* naughty, you don't know." But, of course, it was always emphasized that she was not out of control or overindulged. The *Sunday Dispatch* described her behavior as "Uncurbed without being spoilt."

The article in which this appeared was entitled "The Roguish Princess," the word "roguish" having an endearing quality about it. Once, she was rebuked for using the term "My goodness" within earshot of her mother. Thereafter, if she heard an adult use the expression, as one chronicler put it:

> *... up go her small arms in a gesture of mock amazement, and she presses her palms tightly over her mouth while her blue eyes are full of roguish laughter.*

Normal little girls often have pet names within their family and Elizabeth was no different. At the age of two and a half, having trouble pronouncing her name, she was reportedly calling herself "Tillabet" which she would later change to "Lisabet" or "Lilliebeth." Eventually, she settled on "Lilibet" and this was the name her family have used for her ever since.

Princess Elizabeth as a young girl, at age 3.

In the fall of 1928, she discovered the twin passions that have remained with her since that time—horses and dogs. At the start of the hunting season, she accompanied the Duke and Duchess to Naseby Hall in Northamptonshire which the Duke had rented and they stayed there for most of the winter months. During this time, she developed her love for horses, spending every moment that she could at the stables.

LILIBET AND GRANDPA ENGLAND

There are a great many anecdotes that testify to the feeling that the old and ailing King George V had for his granddaughter Elizabeth. An observer at Sandringham describes His Majesty "chortling with little jokes with her," while the Countess of Airlie explained that:

> *He was fond of his two grandsons, Princess Mary's sons, but Lilibet always came first in his affections. He used to play with her—a thing I never saw him do with his own children—and loved to have her with him.*

Of course, she also had to display appropriate behavior, curtsying to the King and Queen when necessary. In fact, she had learned how to curtsy before the age of 3 and when saying goodnight to her grandfather, always made sure to walk backward toward the door, curtsy and say "I trust Your Majesty will sleep well."

She was particularly upset when he was ill and she was unable to see him. In 1929, she helped "Grandpa England" as she christened him, to get well again after an illness. She spent mornings with the recuperating monarch, cheering him up. The two would sit on chairs at the windows of the house making comments about the passers-by and

it was widely accepted that she had played an important part in helping him to regain his health. In 1930, on her fourth birthday, the King gave Elizabeth a pony, to the delight of the general public.

Their Majesties the King and Queen with the little Princess Elizabeth, at Craigweil House, Bognor.

King George V with Queen Mary and Princess Elizabeth at Craigwell House, Bognor.

THE ROYAL BUBBLE

In August 1930, at Glamis Castle, the Duchess of York gave birth to a second daughter named Margaret Rose (1930 – 2002). The Home Secretary J.R. Clynes (1869 – 1949) who by tradition had to be present for a royal birth, described how when it was announced that the Duchess had given birth:

the countryside was made vivid with the red glow of a hundred bonfires, while sturdy kilted men with flaming torches ran like gnomes from place to place through the darkness.

Margaret Rose's arrival heralded an interesting constitutional question. Elizabeth was next in line after her father, as long as the Prince of Wales did not marry and have a child, but some experts argued that the two sisters, Elizabeth and Margaret Rose, had equal rights to the succession to the throne.

Never before had the question of the precedence of one sister over another arisen. The King, therefore, ordered an enquiry into the matter and the question was resolved in favor of the status quo—Elizabeth had precedence.

But Elizabeth now had someone to play with and the public had another little princess onto which they could project their royal fantasies. People identified with the family living at 145 Piccadilly as the ideal to which everyone should aspire. The father was a quiet, reserved chap, the mother was focused on bringing up her children and the two girls were well-mannered, bright children who were able to fulfill every little girl's fantasy by having ponies and dogs.

All was well in their little bubble. They were looked after by servants and projected confidence in the future. They represented stability and safety, in troubled times with the Nazis coming to power in Germany. Story books were published about them and children from all around the world wrote to them as if they were their friends.

(Above) The Duke and Duchess of York with Princess Elizabeth (right) and Princess Margaret, 1934.
(Left) Just like any family photo, the final version was taken once the girls had settled down.

Marion Crawford

Marion Crawford (1909 – 88), or "Crawfie," as she was known to the royal family, was born into a working-class family in Dunfermline in Fife, Scotland. She had taught at Edinburgh's Moray House Institute before studying child psychology. During this time, she found a summer job as governess to the children of Lord Elgin (1881 – 1968) who was a distant relative of the Duchess of York. In early 1933, she became one of the royal Princesses' governesses and remained with them until Princess Elizabeth was 21 and married Prince Philip.

Following Princess Elizabeth's wedding in 1947, the American magazine, *Ladies' Home Journal*, approached Buckingham Palace and the Foreign Office for stories about the royal family. The Palace refused but the government suggested that they speak to Marion Crawford. The Queen was concerned enough about the approach to warn the former governess not to get involved.

But she did give her approval to Crawfie helping the author of the articles saying, "This would be quite all right as long as your name did not come into it." But when the Queen received a copy of the manuscript for approval, she was horrified. It spoke of the King's moods and the bad relationship the Queen enjoyed with the Duchess of Windsor. She wrote: "The governess has gone off her head." She returned the document with highlighted passages that she would like removed

The editors, however, chose not to show Crawfie the amendments and the article was published as it stood. Marion Crawford went on to write a book, *The Little Princesses*, that sold very well. A column—"Crawfie's Column"—ran in *Woman's Own* although it was actually ghostwritten.

The royal family never spoke to Marion Crawford again and she had to leave her grace and favor home. She retired and bought a house on the road to Balmoral. The royal family often drove past her door, but they never stopped. Following the death of her husband in 1977, she became depressed and attempted suicide. The note she left to be found after her death read: "The world has passed me by and I can't bear those I love to pass me by on the road."

When Marion Crawford died in 1988 at the age of 79, there were no wreaths from the royal family.

CHAPTER 3

THE GATHERING STORM

At last the Duke and Duchess were granted Royal Lodge in Windsor Great Park by the King as their country residence. The Yorks spent many idyllic summers there and the house became important to Princess Elizabeth.

For the Duke of York, however, as a minor royal, there was little to do and although he did make some foreign trips, he undertook nothing again on the scale of the trip to Australia in 1927. Rather, he visited friends and family and

they visited him, he enjoyed gardening, he rode, and he went shooting. This all allowed him to spend time with his family.

Although the Duchess had been a society figure in her youth, fêted for her beauty, the Duke and Duchess now demonstrated very little ambition beyond quietly bringing up their family. As Marion Crawford wrote in her book: "It was a home-like and unpretentious household I found myself in."

Unlike the Duke's brother, the Prince of Wales, they were not a part of the fashionable set of London and had no connection to café society which held little appeal for them. Instead, they delighted in their children and, again as Crawfie reported, everything centered around them. "… each morning began with high jinks in their parents' bedroom." In fact, this daily ritual continued right up until the morning of Princess Elizabeth's wedding day. The end of the day featured similar fun following a bath.

A RATHER PERFUNCTORY EDUCATION

During the day, the Princess received her education under the supervision of Crawfie, she mostly spent her time learning English, French, and history, an education described as "wide, rather than deep." There were no examinations and no classmates against whom to pit her learning. Furthermore, her teacher taught all three subjects and Crawfie had little more than a training college diploma to support her efforts.

It is worth saying, however, that at the time, it was not at all unusual for young women

H.R.H. THE PRINCE OF WALES
ELIZABETH.

Princess Elizabeth with her uncle Edward when he was Prince of Wales, 1935.

born into the upper classes to be educated at home in this rather perfunctory way. The Duke and Duchess were determined that their children should not be intellectual and with only seven and a half hours' education a week, it was unlikely that they would become so. Even Crawfie had to concede, however, that the girls were unlikely to play significant roles in the future and their parents were merely providing them with memories of a happy childhood.

Queen Mary, however, was less casual about the girls' education, demanding a timetable of lessons and insisting that Princess Elizabeth should read the very best children's literature. In fact, she often chose what the Princess should read. She devised "instructive amusements" for the children. These included such things as a visit to the Tower of London.

THE DUKE OF YORK'S CAMP

The Duke of York always took great interest in the plight of poor urban children, languishing in inner-city slums and industrial towns. He was President of the Industrial Welfare Association which organized projects to help working-class young people. His name was used in the Duke of York's Camp through which, every year, a hundred public schools and a hundred industrial enterprises were asked to send two boys each to a summer camp.

The idea was that everyone would be treated equally and everyone, from no matter which side of the tracks, should mingle and socialize. Robert Hyde who organized the summer camp, indicated that the aim of the project was to "tame young Bolshevists." The Duke of York attended each year for a couple of days, dressing casually and joining in the campfire songs and games. When the last camp was held in 1939, Princess Elizabeth and Princess Margaret Rose also came along and joined in.

That was really about as far as the Princess got with socializing. There was a rumor at one point that she was going to be sent to a girls' boarding school or to a preparatory school but there was no truth in it. One report suggested that the Duchess was the one who wanted Princess Elizabeth to go to school but after consultation with the King and Queen and the Government Cabinet, it was decided that she would not go after all.

There were actually reports that during his brief reign, Edward VIII was against his niece going to school and this view was bolstered by the suggestion that the late King George V had also vetoed her attendance. There was also concern that if one school was picked, all the others would be jealous. There were concerns, too, about her mixing with the wrong kind of schoolmates.

Edward, Prince of Wales (center) with his brother the Duke of York (right) and the Duke's children, Princess Elizabeth and Princess Margaret, 1935.

TWO VERY DISTINCTIVE SISTERS

Elizabeth and Margaret Rose were different to each other. Eventually, the roguish quality that the older Princess had portrayed when younger faded, especially as it became clear that she would have a significant role to play in the nation's history. She became more serious as her destiny became clear. She was said by one observer to have a "serious turn of mind" and "was quiet, unassuming, and friendly, yet she has inherited a dignity which properly becomes her position."

Margaret, on the other hand, was artistic and liked music. She was an amusing and rather talented mimic. Elizabeth would be critical of "her sister's instinct for burlesque, while secretly enjoying it." They were presented to the public as two different characters, one serious and responsible, the other whimsical and capricious.

Still, the two were girls of whom both their parents and the nation could be proud. The diplomat Miles Lampson wrote of Elizabeth in his diary in 1934: "I have seldom seen such an enchanting child as Princess Elizabeth."

They were central to the jubilee of 70-year-old King George V in 1935. By this time, the old King was revered by his people. Receiving their adulation, he said: "I cannot understand it, after all I am only a very ordinary sort of fellow." Princess Lilibet who was 9 years old rode in a carriage alongside him, accepting the cheers of the crowds lining the streets.

THE END OF A REIGN

By Christmas, the King was ailing and his voice was weak and croaky as he delivered his radio broadcast to his subjects all around the world. At Sandringham, where the royal family spent the festive season, he was noticeably short of breath when walking and was forced to stop every hundred yards or so. Once again, it seems, his Lilibet brought him some comfort.

The King was not the only one in the royal family who was ill. The Duchess of York had been suffering from pneumonia, but by January 17 when the Princesses returned home to Royal Lodge, she was much better. On January 20, the King took a turn for the worse and the Duke was summoned to Sandringham. The King died that day surrounded by his family. His body was brought back to London where it lay in state, hundreds of thousands of his subjects filing past his coffin. On the night before the funeral, the late King's four sons stood at the corners of the catafalque, dressed in military uniform. Grandpa England's funeral took place on January 28, 1936.

King George V and Queen Mary celebrate their Silver Jubilee in 1935 on the balcony at Buckingham Palace. The young Princesses Margaret and Elizabeth can be seen in the center.

AN UNPRECEDENTED CRISIS

The Palace was in pandemonium at the prospect of a new King, especially one as different in nature and behavior as Edward VIII, as he chose to call himself. Courtiers and officials worried for their futures and a new informality emerged as old, ingrained customs were broken down. Queen Mary moved out of Buckingham Palace and took up residence at Marlborough House in St. James's. The Yorks now moved one step closer to the crown and their relative anonymity was about to end. Interest increased not only in the Duke, but inevitably also in his 9-year-old daughter, Elizabeth.

There were mutterings about the new King and a huge amount of speculation as to whether he would ever marry and have children. Even the Archbishop of Canterbury joined in the gossip:

> *The children—Lilibet, Margaret Rose, and Margaret Elphinstone (1925 – 2016)—joined us. They sang some action-songs most charmingly. It was strange to think of the destiny which might be awaiting the little Elizabeth, at present second from the Throne. She and her lively little sister are certainly most entrancing children.*

Life continued as before, although, of course, they now saw much less of their Uncle David—as they called the new King—than previously. The Duke and Duchess were obviously aware of the constitutional storm that was brewing but they continued to indulge their interests of gardening, riding, and embroidery, and visited friends as before.

EDWARD AND MRS. SIMPSON

There were rumors about the couple but nothing made it into print. It was believed by editors and newspaper proprietors that to print a story about Edward and Mrs. Simpson would certainly provide a welcome boost in sales, but it would be merely a short-term one and was not worth it. In fact, they feared that it would result in a backlash from readers. Scandalous news involving a member of the royal family was at the time strictly off-limits.

An abdication was a terrible prospect, damaging to the constitution and creating an unprecedented crisis. The Duke of York was depressed by the possibility that his brother would step down and he would be thrust onto the stage to replace him. Rumors spread that the Duke was refusing to countenance the prospect of being King and that Queen Mary had already agreed to act as regent for Princess Elizabeth.

In the American press it was even suggested that the Duke of York's stammer was a symptom of epilepsy. The private secretary to Edward VIII, and later to the Duke as King, Alan "Tommy" Lascelles (1887 – 1981), wrote in his diary that he feared that in the event of an abdication the Duke of York might suffer a breakdown.

The granting of a divorce *decree nisi* to Wallis Simpson on October 27, 1936, increased the tension felt by the royal family. Writing to a courtier a month later, the Duke of York said:

> *If the worst happens & I have to take over, you can be assured that I will do my best to clear up the inevitable mess, if the whole fabric does not crumble under the shock and strain of it all.*

The Year of the Three Kings. King Edward VIII (right) and his brother, the Duke of York, the future King George VI, walk solemnly in the funeral procession of King George V, 1936.

Mrs. Wallis Simpson

Bessie Wallis Warfield (1896 – 1986) was born in Blue Ridge Summit, Pennsylvania, USA. Her father died a few months later and she and her mother moved to Baltimore in 1901. Seven years later Mrs. Warfield married the son of a Democratic Party boss.

In 1916, Wallis married Earl Winfield Spencer Jr. (1888 – 1950), a United States Navy pilot. He was transferred to a training base in San Diego and was commanding officer there until 1921. Their marriage ran into difficulties and after several separations, he was posted to the Far East while Wallis remained in the United States. At the time, she was having an affair with an Argentine diplomat.

In 1924, she was reunited with her husband in the Far East, but in Beijing during a tour of China, Wallis met and had another affair with Count Galeazzo Ciano (1903 – 44) who later became Italian Foreign Minister. As a result of this affair, it was rumored that Wallis fell pregnant and a bungled abortion left her unable to have children. She and her husband divorced in 1927.

In 1928, Wallis married a divorced Anglo-American shipping executive, Ernest Aldrich Simpson (1897 – 1958), and lived in London. In 1931, Wallis was introduced to the Prince of Wales by his then mistress Thelma, Lady Furness (1904 – 70), and three years later, when Lady Furness was overseas, Wallis replaced her in the Prince's affections.

The Prince steadfastly denied his relationship but staff reported seeing the two in bed together. He fell hopelessly in love with her, a biographer describing him as "slavishly dependent" upon her. He gave her money and jewels and in February 1935 the pair holidayed in Europe.

Following the death of King George V in 1936, the Prince of Wales became King for a short time, but decided to abdicate so he could be with the woman he loved. On June 3, 1937, the couple were married in France and became known as the Duke and Duchess of Windsor. They remained married until Edward's death 35 years later.

Wallis Simpson died at age 89, on April 24, 1986.

Edward VIII

Born Edward Albert Christian George Andrew Patrick David on June 23, 1894, the future Edward VIII was the oldest son of the Duke and Duchess of York, later King George V and Queen Mary. At the time of his birth, he was third in line of succession to the throne. Initially tutored at home, he entered Osborne Naval College in 1907 and two years later enrolled at the Royal Naval College at Dartmouth. When his father ascended the throne in May 1910, David, as he was known to his family, became Duke of Cornwall and Duke of Rothesay. A month later, he was invested as Prince of Wales and Earl of Chester. He was withdrawn immediately from his naval course and went to Magdalen College, Oxford. After eight terms, he left Oxford with no academic qualifications.

At the outbreak of World War I, Edward joined the Grenadier Guards but was prevented from serving at the front, despite wishing to do so. He visited the front line to see trench warfare and gained a great deal of respect from veterans of the war. After the war, he often represented his father at home and abroad, his charm and good looks and the fact that he remained unmarried, made him a hugely popular figure. He visited many poverty-stricken areas of Great Britain, showing compassion to the people he met.

He had several affairs during this time, including a relationship with a Parisian courtesan, Marguerite Alibert (1890 – 1971). He broke up with Alibert in 1918 in order to begin a new relationship with a married woman, the textile heiress, Freda Dudley Ward (1894 – 1983). His womanizing was of concern to the government and to his father who said presciently of him: "After I am dead, the boy will ruin himself in 12 months."

In 1934, Edward began a relationship with the twice-divorced Wallis Simpson, sowing the seeds for the Abdication Crisis of 1936, when he became King on January 20 and abdicated on December 11 the same year. With a reign of 326 days, Edward is one of the shortest-reigning monarchs in British history. After his abdication, he was created Duke of Windsor, and following accusations of Nazi sympathies during World War II, he spent the rest of his life in retirement in France. He died at his home in Paris in 1972, at age 77.

Edward VIII (1894 – 1972) was King of the United Kingdom and the Dominions of the British Empire, and Emperor of India from January 20, 1936. Edward was never crowned as King, abdicating on December 11, 1936, before his Coronation.

THE ABDICATION CRISIS

Wallis Simpson was introduced to King George V and Queen Elizabeth by the Prince of Wales at Buckingham Palace in 1935 as the woman he proposed to marry, but later they refused to receive her. There was concern among the government and prominent establishment figures about the influence that an American divorcee with something of a questionable past might have over the Prince of Wales both then and later as King.

The couple were subject to surveillance by the Special Branch of the Metropolitan Police who reported back on their relationship and investigated the private life of Wallis Simpson. They reported that at the same time as having a relationship with the Prince of Wales, she was also seeing a car salesman named Guy Trundle.

She was viewed by the establishment as a gold-digger, an unscrupulous woman who was pursuing the Prince for his money. There was also, undoubtedly, antipathy toward the United States in the inter-war years and many Britons were unhappy at the thought of an American queen.

A DEAFENING SILENCE

When the Prince of Wales became King, her name began to appear regularly in the Court Circular, as she attended more functions with the King, but the name of her husband was conspicuously absent. A holiday that the two spent in the eastern Mediterranean was widely covered by the world's press, but did not appear in British newspapers. When Wallis filed for divorce at the end of October 1936, speculation was rife in the American media that the King would marry her as soon as she was free of her marriage to Ernest Simpson.

Around this time, the King received a letter from his private secretary warning him that "The silence in the British press on the subject of Your Majesty's friendship with Mrs. Simpson is not going to be maintained ... Judging by the letters from British subjects living in foreign countries where the press has been outspoken, the effect will be calamitous." It is believed that this letter was probably drafted with the help of British government ministers.

THE PRYING EYES OF THE PRESS

On November 16, Edward invited Prime Minister Stanley Baldwin (1867 – 1947) to Buckingham Palace to give him the news that he would, indeed, be marrying Wallis Simpson. Baldwin insisted, however, that as she would become

The Duke of Windsor, formerly King Edward VIII, with Mrs. Wallis Simpson, Chateau de Cande, near Tours, France, 1937.

queen, the opinion of the people must be listened to. Still, however, the British press maintained its silence on the matter. This changed following a speech by Alfred Blunt, Bishop of Bradford (1879 – 1957) in which he referred to the King's need for Divine Grace:

> First, on the faith, prayer, and self-dedication of the King himself; and on that it would be improper for me to say anything except to commend him to God's grace, which he will so abundantly need, as we all need it—for the King is a man like ourselves—if he is to do his duty faithfully. We hope that he is aware of his need. Some of us wish that he gave more positive signs of such awareness.

This was the first time anyone had spoken publicly about the situation and the press leapt on it, at last removing the barriers to talking about the monarch's private life. The speech was front page news the following day. Bizarrely, the bishop claimed he had never heard of Wallis Simpson when he made the speech, but it was too late. Mrs. Simpson immediately headed for the south of France, removing herself from the prying eyes of the press.

THE ONLY OPTION

Baldwin warned Edward that were he to marry Mrs. Simpson against the government's advice, it would resign *en masse*. Edward told a surprised Prime Minister that if the government was so opposed then he would abdicate. A morganatic marriage was an option—they would marry but she would not be queen although she would enjoy a title of some kind. It had happened in Europe before, but there was no precedent for a morganatic marriage in Britain.

When consulted, the leaders of the Dominions—Australia, Canada, New Zealand, South Africa, and the Irish Free State—agreed that the only option was abdication. The leaders of the British opposition parties concurred but Winston Churchill (1874 – 1965) argued for a delay in the hope that the King would fall out of love with Mrs. Simpson.

Support for him came from the working class and ex-servicemen while the middle and upper classes were outraged. Finally, on December 5, the King conceded defeat and five days later he signed the necessary documents, witnessed by his three younger brothers—the Duke of York, Duke of Gloucester, and Duke of Kent.

The *Daily Express* front page reporting the abdication of King Edward VIII, 1936.

ABDICATION AND CORONATION

THE STORM FINALLY BREAKS

At the beginning of December, the news broke and Mrs. Simpson's name filled the headlines of the nation's newspapers. The Duke of York was beside himself. He wrote how he had a meeting with his mother on December 9 to discuss the inevitability of an abdication: "... when I told her what had happened ... I broke down and sobbed like a child." He later described watching his brother sign away his crown:

> I ... was present at the fateful moment which made me D's successor to the Throne. Perfectly calm D signed 5 or 6 copies of the instrument of Abdication & then 5 copies of his message to Parliament, one for each Dominion Parliament. It was a dreadful moment & one never to be forgotten by those present ... I went to R.L. [Royal Lodge] for a rest ... But I could not rest alone & returned to the Fort [Fort Belvedere in Surrey, country home of Edward VIII] at 5.45. Wigram [Private Secretary to Edward VIII] was present at a terrible lawyer interview ... I later went to London where I found a large crowd outside my house cheering madly. I was overwhelmed.

The Duke of York, an unassuming, quiet man who had previously enjoyed life away from the spotlight, along with his devoted wife, shunned the bright lights and the café society his brother loved so much, was now King. For the next few days he was guided through the ceremonials of monarchy by his court.

Crawfie reported that after being hugged by his daughters he left, his face "pale and haggard" for his first Privy Council meeting, dressed in the uniform of an Admiral of the Fleet. His life had changed irrevocably, but so had the life of his daughter Princess Elizabeth, now next in line to the throne.

It took just six days to see one king off the throne and another onto it—an astonishing achievement, especially as it was all handled so decorously. There was no establishment of a "King's party" to lobby on behalf of Edward VIII, no appeal to the British public for support. Neither was there any political infighting or point-scoring, nor invective from within the ranks of the royal family itself. That did not mean, however, that it was not a significant historical moment as well as an important turning-point for the way in which the British royal family was perceived.

It may have been the behavior of Queen Victoria and Prince Albert that did it, but the private lives of the royals were viewed as being beyond reproach. Of course, Edward VII had let standards slip a little as had his son, the Duke of Clarence (Prince Albert Victor, 1864–92) but not since the nineteenth century had it been a matter of constitutional importance.

CHANGING PERSPECTIVES

What was clear at the end of it all was that the people had to give their permission for the monarch to reign and that Parliament was paramount in this. The Abdication was a very big moment; not since 1688 had Parliament removed a king because he was unsuitable.

The situation was summed up by the charismatic Scottish leader of the left-wing

Independent Labour Party, James Maxton (1885 – 1946) who famously said in the House of Commons: "All the King's horses and all the King's men couldn't put Humpty-Dumpty together again." It was all different and no longer would it be possible for the monarch to maintain a position of moral authority, to make interventions where necessary from the vantage point of one who was outside of politics.

The job of George VI was to reassure the people, to provide stability and caution, and persuade them to put the events of 1936 behind them. He was well-positioned with his wife and children to do this. Edward VIII had recognized this in a farewell radio address to the nation:

> *This decision has been made less difficult to me by the sure knowledge that my brother, with his long training in the public affairs of this country and with his fine qualities, will be able to take my place forthwith without interruption or injury to the life and progress of the empire. And he has one matchless blessing, enjoyed by so many of you, and not bestowed on me—a happy home with his wife and children.*

A GUIDING LIGHT

The scandalous behavior of Wallis Simpson contrasted greatly with the two Princesses living at 145 Piccadilly. They represented purity and simplicity, and to many, Princess Elizabeth was a guiding light shining on the future. Now 10 years old, she was reported to have "great charm and a natural unassuming dignity." Lady Strathmore said that when she was told she could be Queen, she said she was "ardently praying for a brother."

Her mother was, after all, only 36 when her husband became King and there was still time for her to have another child. But gradually, the nation began to accept that it was likely that a queen would follow George VI. Some even speculated that she would be named Princess of Wales. Princess Margaret recalled asking her after their father became King, "Does that mean you're going to be Queen?" "Yes, I suppose it does," came the answer.

Princess Elizabeth is reported by Crawfie to have been horrified at the thought of moving to Buckingham Palace. Crawfie herself disliked living there. "Camping in a museum" was how she described it. They soon made it home though, and Elizabeth moved into a schoolroom that overlooked the palace lawns. The biggest change was that the family was now firmly in the public eye, especially in the build-up to the King's Coronation.

THE STUTTERING DUKE OF YORK

When the Princesses looked out of the palace windows they were greeted by a crowd that never diminished. Meanwhile, the King was engaged in welcoming visitors, having meetings and attending functions. The Queen was similarly preoccupied. Princess Elizabeth was now accompanied by a detective wherever she went. The Queen insisted on the formalities of monarchy being observed and the Princesses no longer referred to their parents as Mummy and Papa, but as the King and the Queen. Even in the nursery, meals were served by two footmen in scarlet livery.

Naturally, the main pressure and the greatest changes fell on the King's shoulders. His speech impediment was the cause of much anxiety for him, especially when making speeches which he was increasingly called on to do. It went unmentioned by the British newspapers but in the American press he had become known as "the stuttering Duke of York." The principal concern was how he would perform at his Coronation.

CORONATION DAY

There was much sympathy for the new King. Kingsley Martin (1897 – 1969), editor of the *New Statesman* attempted to sum up the feelings about the King of a typical member of the British public:

We would still prefer to cheer Edward, but we know that we've got to cheer George. After all, it's Edward's fault that he's not on the throne, and George didn't ask to get there. He's only doing his duty, and it's up to us to show that we appreciate it.

For Britain the Coronation was a vitally important moment and not just in healing the wound of the Abdication. It was perceived to symbolize liberty at a time when fascism's orchestrated parades were being seen in Europe. It was "a pageant more splendid than any dictators can put on," as one commentator noted, "beating Rome and Nuremberg hollow at their own bewildering best, and with no obverse side of compulsion or horror." The power and wealth of Britain and British Imperial might would be on show for the world to wonder at.

Naturally, this piled even more pressure on the central character in this imperial drama—the new King George VI. He was terrified, telling the former Prime Minister Ramsay MacDonald (1866–1937) afterward that during the ceremony he was pretty much unaware of what was going on. It went well, however, the Princesses watching intently from the royal box alongside their grandmother, Queen Mary.

Princess Elizabeth was prepared for the ceremony by her governess who read to her from Queen Victoria's account of her own coronation in 1837 which began: "I was awoken by the guns in Hyde Park and could not get much sleep afterwards on account of the people, bands etc."

ON A COLD AND MISTY MORNING

The Princess wrote her own account, dedicated to her mother and father. Like Queen Victoria, she was woken at 5 a.m. but by a band playing outside her window, not guns. She described how with her nursemaid Bobo MacDonald "we

crouched in the window looking on to a cold, misty morning." The Princesses ate breakfast and then, according to Elizabeth's account:

[We] showed ourselves to the visitors and housemaids. Now I shall try and give you a description of our dresses. They were white silk with old cream lace and had little gold bows all the way down the middle. They had puffed sleeves with one little bow in the center. Then there were the robes of purple velvet with gold on the edge.

We went along to Mummy's bedroom and found her putting on her dress. Papa was dressed in a white shirt, breeches and stockings, and over this he wore a crimson satin coat. Then a page came and said it was time to go down, so we kissed Mummy, and wished her good luck and went down. There we said good morning to Aunt Alice, Aunt Marina and Aunt Mary with whom we were to drive to the Abbey. We were then told to get into the carriage … At first it was very jolty but we soon got used to it.

It must have been an extraordinary experience for the two little girls to see their parents being crowned King and Queen but there were moments of lightness too. Princess Elizabeth wrote:

At the end the service got rather boring as it was all prayers. Grannie and I were looking to see how many pages to the end, and we turned one more and then I pointed to the word at the bottom of the page and it said "Finis." We both smiled at each other and turned back to the service.

THE CENTER OF ATTENTION

Princess Elizabeth was being given more of a role in royal activities, attending the lavish garden parties with thousands of guests that were held every year in the grounds of Buckingham Palace. She also played her part in children's pony shows and presented trophies at the Bath Club where she and her sister swam occasionally. At the age of 13 she became president of the Children's League of the Princess Elizabeth of York Hospital.

She spent time meeting and dining with dignitaries and she was expected to be able to converse with them at the dinner table. Her mother helped her in this by role-playing, pretending to be a statesman or religious figure.

She and her sister were also taught how to manage being continually on show, the center of attention for thousands of people at a garden party, for instance, and how to walk at a steady, measured pace.

Her mother also guided their faith, reading bible stories to the Princesses and instructing them in the Book of Common Prayer. George Carey (born 1935), the 103rd Archbishop of

King George VI and his wife Queen Elizabeth on the day of their Coronation, May 12, 1937, with their daughters Princess Margaret and Princess Elizabeth.

Canterbury, reckons that "The Queen knows the prayer book backwards." Queen Elizabeth, the Queen Mother knelt in prayer every night and it is thought that her daughter also does this.

Tempers and moods were strictly forbidden. It has been said that Princess Elizabeth shared the hot temper and mood swings of her father, George V, and Edward VII, but the Queen soon calmed this part of her nature. She once wrote to Princess Elizabeth: "never shout or frighten" or "you lose their delightful trust in you." "Remember to keep your temper & your word & be loving."

EDUCATING ELIZABETH

In 1938, Henry Marten (1872 – 1948), Vice-Provost of Eton began teaching Princess Elizabeth constitutional history at Eton College. Marten's task was to remind the Princess of the tradition of which she was an important part as well as instructing her on the changes that had been introduced. He recalled teaching her that apart from the Papacy, the British monarchy was the longest-surviving in the world, stretching back more than a millennium.

Marten also taught Elizabeth that the secret of the survival of the monarchy was its ability to adapt to changing circumstances. He took her through the 1931 Statute of Westminster, explaining how it had established the British Commonwealth by rendering the allegiance to the Crown the only surviving link that connected Britain and her Dominions. He also spoke about the challenges and opportunities that had been brought by the advent of broadcasting which enabled the monarch to speak to all of his or her people at one time through the medium of the airwaves.

As well as Marten, Princess Elizabeth was later taught by the Vicomtesse de Bellaigue who gave instruction in French, French Literature, and European History. Ever-anxious to avoid their daughter becoming too intellectual, or

even viewed as such, the King and Queen were at pains to let it be known that she was having cookery lessons in the kitchens at Royal Lodge.

WATCHING THE WORLD GO BY

The Princess had also learned how to clean a house, picking up the rudiments of sweeping, dusting, and polishing. Somewhat bizarrely it was said that Queen Mary was "a keen housewife" and that she had been impressed by the Princess's domestic skills.

Relatively mature for her age, she was still comparatively shy at the age of 13. She was always seeking the support of Crawfie who recalled her as lonely and shut-off from the world. Elizabeth would stand for hours at the window of the palace watching the world go by and asking Crawfie questions about what went on beyond the palace walls.

She later told the artist Pietro Annigoni (1910 – 88) when he was painting her portrait in Buckingham Palace's Yellow Drawing Room how, as a child, she had spent hours gazing out of the windows:

I loved watching the people and the cars there in the Mall. They all seemed so busy. I used to wonder what they were doing and where they were all going, and what they thought about outside the Palace.

THE TRANSATLANTIC CROSSING

Monarchy really earns its keep during wartime or even when there are just rumors of war, as was the case in the late 1930s. The King and Queen were important propaganda devices for the British government but were also wheeled out to greet ambassadors and politicians from around the world.

In general, the children remained at home although one exception was in the fall of 1938 when the 12-year-old Princess Elizabeth accompanied the Queen to Clydeside for the launch of the Cunard ship, *Queen Elizabeth*. When the King and Queen traveled abroad, it was never considered that it might be beneficial to the girls' education to travel with them. Thus, the Princess was left behind staring out of the palace windows and wondering about the world outside.

In July 1938, the King and Queen undertook a hugely successful visit to France. There was a political point to the visit—it was intended to strengthen the alliance between Great Britain and France. Following the success of that visit, the government decided that it would be a good idea to send the royal couple to North America, to strengthen ties there. Ties that would be essential in the event of war in Europe.

President Franklin D. Roosevelt (1882 – 1945) extended an invitation to the Princesses, but King George graciously declined. The Canadian part of the visit was going to be particularly taxing and he and his wife did not think their children would be up to it.

CHAOS IN EUROPE

Europe was in a ferment by May 1939 when the King and Queen embarked for Canada. The Spanish Civil War had been raging since 1936, and troops of the right-wing General Francisco Franco (1892 – 1975) had captured Madrid. Meanwhile, on March 15, Adolf Hitler, the German Chancellor had ordered the German Army into Prague and Bohemia, and Moravia was declared a German protectorate. War seemed inevitable which made the royal tour all the more important.

But as the royal couple prepared to leave, attention swung away from the approach of war to the two young Princesses boarding their parents' ship to say farewell. It was noted that Princess Elizabeth had grown and was almost as tall as her mother. She was dressed differently too, sporting a tilted cap and the hem of her coat and dress was down below her knees.

The girls were understandably sad, one observer remarking that "they looked somewhat forlorn" as the liner sailed out of the harbor. Meanwhile, on deck, the King and Queen gazed back at them until they were out of sight.

WHEN RESISTANCE NEARLY GOES

The King and Queen spent three weeks in Canada and were guests of Roosevelt in the United States. While they were away, the Princesses kept details of their progress in North America using maps pinned up in their schoolroom. The Queen wrote often, saying on one occasion that Americans were "particularly easy and pleasant ... and delighted to find that we were ordinary & fairly polite people with a big job of work." She did also mention how stressful it could be to be "almost continually on show ... there comes a moment when one's resistance nearly goes."

In return Princess Elizabeth sent photographs across the Atlantic and she also sent a film of Princess Margaret and all their pets made using a cine-camera. Queen Mary, meanwhile, organized outings and visits for the girls to take their minds off their parents' absence. They went to the Bank of England and toured the vaults, accompanied by Governor Montagu Norman (1871 – 1950).

Unfortunately, such visits always seemed to come to the attention of the media who turned them into royal spectacles. After one visit to London Zoo that was covered extensively in the press, the Palace became concerned. The King's Assistant Private Secretary, Sir Eric Miéville (1896 – 1971) wrote:

> *What happens now is that by some extraordinary means, unknown to me, whenever they are due to visit an institution, news always leaks out ahead to certain members of the press ... One has to remember that in these days such information given to the newspapers is worth money.*

CHAPTER 5

COMING OF AGE

Compared to other European royal families, the British royal family had an excellent war, emerging from it stronger and more popular than ever. The consternation and doubt of Edward VIII's abdication were consigned to history. It was difficult, however. The tight family bond that had existed pre-war was challenged due to the separations that were necessary. However, the King became a symbol not just of nationhood, but of hope and a bastion against fear.

He could have no effect on the conduct of the war, or on the outcome, but he served in the best way he was able, as did his wife. The Princesses were, in a way, frozen in time, especially as their whereabouts during the conflict were always shrouded in mystery. If they were photographed, it was always against a neutral backdrop so that no one could work out where they were.

With the situation rapidly deteriorating—war was declared on September 3, 1939. King George returned to London from the family's summer holiday at Balmoral on August 23. The Queen arrived back on August 28. The Princesses did not join them, however. They were sent instead to Birkhall, another estate on Royal Deeside in Scotland that had been purchased by Prince Albert. There they were looked after by a retinue of servants as well as several police officers.

SLEEPING IN THE DUNGEONS

Their education continued, Henry Marten sending them work and Princess Elizabeth posting back to him her written papers for comment and correction. At Christmas they went to Sandringham and after that they spent the remainder of the period known as the "Phoney War" at Royal Lodge. Both at Birkhall and at Royal Lodge there were Girl Guides meetings, and the Princesses mixed with evacuees from London's East End. This was a rare contact indeed with the working-class children from the city.

Prime Minister Neville Chamberlain (1869 – 1940) was forced to resign on May 10, 1940, and was replaced by the indomitable Winston Churchill. On the same day the German army invaded the Low Countries (Belgium, Luxembourg, and the Netherlands). The Princesses were moved to Windsor Castle and they spent much of the remainder of the war there. They slept in the castle dungeons, out of reach of German bombs but it was not too bad and, in fact, Princess Margaret later recalled this period as providing some of the happiest memories of her childhood.

Their circumstances were much less formal. They ate in the State Dining Room, for instance, with their governesses and officers of the Grenadier Guards who were providing security for them. The King and Queen were with them to begin with, traveling to London as necessary, but as the war progressed they began to spend the weekdays in London and the weekends at Windsor.

GOOD LUCK TO YOU ALL

The girls were presented as the center of a family that was suffering the privations of war as much as anyone. So when Elizabeth delivered her first broadcast on October 13, 1940, it was mainly aimed at British children who had been evacuated to North America, although the true intention of the broadcast was to influence American opinion in favor of entering the conflict. Her words echoed across the Atlantic and around the world:

All of us children who are still at home, think continually of our friends and relations who have gone overseas—who have traveled thousands of miles to find a wartime home and a kindly welcome in Canada, Australia, New Zealand, South Africa, and the United States of America.

One journalist writing after the war recalled that "The King rushed into the room after the first rehearsal exclaiming to me, '*She's* exactly like *her!*' meaning the Princess's voice was extraordinarily like that of the Queen, and everyone knows how excellently the Queen broadcasts."

At the end of the broadcast, Princess Margaret was introduced. Elizabeth told listeners: "My sister is by my side, and we are both going to say good night to you. Come on, Margaret." "Good night," Margaret replied. "Good night and good luck to you all."

A STAR IN THE DARKNESS

It was a sign of how badly the war was going at the time and how important it was that American opinion be changed because until then the King and Queen had declined all such invitations for the Princess to broadcast. The British ambassador to the United States dismissed such requests as "stunts" and the Palace insisted that "there is, of course, no question of the Princesses broadcasting, nor is it likely to be considered for many years to come."

It was a huge success on both sides of the Atlantic, a brilliant star in the bleak darkness of the time. It was splashed across the front pages of American newspapers and radio stations' switchboards were jammed by listeners demanding that the broadcast be repeated. The BBC made it into a gramophone record for sale in America and in the British Empire.

Princess Margaret (left) and Princess Elizabeth broadcasting to the children of the empire, October 13, 1940.

LOOKING THE EAST END IN THE FACE

If the Princesses were to be identified with the displaced children of Great Britain, it also seemed like smart thinking to portray their parents as ordinary Londoners who did not let the bombs of the German Blitz prevent them getting on with their lives. They could identify with Londoners in one way, certainly, because on September 13, 1940, Buckingham Palace was hit by a bomb.

The Queen Mother said that she was removing an eyelash from the King's eye when they heard "the unmistakable whirr-whirr of a German plane" followed by the "scream of a bomb." She wrote:

> *It all happened so quickly, that we had only time to look foolishly at each other when the scream hurtled past us and exploded with a tremendous crash in the quadrangle.*

The bomb destroyed the palace chapel but it was a defining moment for the royal family. They were seen walking amid the rubble just as ordinary Londoners were doing. The Queen said:

> *Now we can look the East End in the face.*

They had been advised by the Foreign Office to leave Britain but had steadfastly refused. The Queen expressed the family's complete resolve:

> *The children will not leave unless I do. I shall not leave unless their father does, and the King will not leave the country in any circumstances, whatever.*

ADAPTING TO AUSTERITY

The King adapted brilliantly to the rigors of war. From being a stuttering wreck who had not looked as if he would be able to get through his own Coronation, he now looked made for the job of being a war-time sovereign. All the same, his job did not amount to much. He and the Queen visited bombed-out areas where they would be photographed, he attended public ceremonies and he bestowed honors and medals. He also received visitors and was adept, as were the other members of his family, at putting people at their ease.

The Queen could make a person to whom she was talking feel like the only person in the world with whom she wished to converse at

On April 23, 1941, King George VI and Queen Elizabeth met air raid victims in the East End of London. Due to her indomitable spirit and morale boosting visits to London's bombed streets during the war, German leader Adolf Hitler described Queen Elizabeth as "the most dangerous woman in Europe."

that particular moment. The end result was a kind of shared affection between visitor and royal family. Queen Alexandra of Yugoslavia decided after meeting them in 1944 that: "... this was the sort of home life I wanted, with children and dogs playing at my feet." The King's limitations—he was described as "a plodder" by one Gentleman Usher—now worked to his advantage and he was imbued with decent ordinariness.

The royal family stuck to the austere rules that governed ordinary people's lives. Thus, there was an announcement that for Princess Elizabeth's fourteenth birthday, the three-tiered birthday cake would be made of plain sponge. It was all genuine, however, and Eleanor Roosevelt (1884 – 1962), on her late 1942 visit to the palace discovered that the restrictions were being rigorously applied in terms of food, heating, and water usage. Broken windows had even been replaced with wooden panels.

THE DUKE OF BEAUFORT'S HOUNDS

Of course, the royal family still had the opportunity to disappear to Windsor at the weekend and continued to holiday at Balmoral and Sandringham. The Princesses, too, continued with their riding lessons. Princess Elizabeth learned to ride side-saddle and twice during the war she won the trophy for the driving of a "utility vehicle" at the Royal Windsor Horse Show.

Elizabeth shot her first stag in October 1942 at Balmoral and in 1943 she hunted with the Garth Hounds, later riding with the Duke of Beaufort's Hounds in Gloucestershire. These were not activities open to the ordinary Londoner, but the decision to let her participate in them was said to be "in accord with the general policy of making her life as 'normal' as possible."

There were several royal balls at which the King was able to demonstrate his prowess as a dancer. The 15-year-old Princess Elizabeth went to her first in July 1941, dancing a few times with her father, watched by the royal family and their guests. Later, dances were held every two weeks in Buckingham Palace's Bow Room.

FIVE SHILLINGS A WEEK

It was necessary for the cocooned life of the royal family to be breached in order to maximize their propaganda value. Numerous photographs of them going about their daily life appeared in magazines and newspapers and in newsreels in cinemas. These emphasized that the war had made little difference to the traditional British way of life.

The Princesses were photographed working in the garden at Royal Lodge, "digging for victory," as one of the government slogans of the time put it. They were a self-contained unit, as was evident from photographs that would find their way out onto the front line of the war as well as to those laboring away in Britain, contributing to the war effort. The girls were the paradigms of what a young girl should be in war time—conscientious, caring, and dignified, but also deeply interested in what was going on in the war.

Elizabeth was employed to demonstrate support for government schemes. She was shown digging for victory as well as knitting for it. In order to raise funds to buy wool so that they could continue knitting, they organized a concert for the King and Queen and members of the armed forces that raised around £70.

A great deal of publicity was given when the Princesses were immunized against diphtheria, publicizing the government's efforts to get all children vaccinated. Princess Elizabeth was delegated to award the prize to the best essay by a Welsh schoolchild on the subject of metal salvage.

Even Elizabeth's pocket money was discussed in public. A story ran that she received only five shillings a week, despite receiving an annual Civil List payment of £6,000. But even then, half of the five shillings was donated to good causes supporting the war effort. A "Princess Elizabeth Day" was announced during which money was collected for donation to children's charities.

SINGLE-MINDED INTELLIGENCE

Being drawn into the war effort was for the Princess little different to the experiences of every other young person in wartime Britain. Children left school and were taken straight into war work or entered the armed services. Nonetheless, it was a strange time for the Princesses and many would have been overwhelmed by the range of public duties in which they had to be engaged at such a young age.

But they took it all in their stride, especially Elizabeth who comes across in the accounts of those who encountered her as a reserved, strong-willed girl without aesthetic or intellectual pursuits to distract her. Single-minded she may have been but she also displayed intelligence, a quality attested to by both the Archbishop of Canterbury and Eleanor Roosevelt who each engaged in serious conversation with her.

Nonetheless, she seemed young for her age and, in fact, remained so for some years well into her teens.

COLONEL OF THE GRENADIER GUARDS

Adulthood was approaching and as it did, Princess Elizabeth's duties increased. In January 1942, after the death of the Duke of Connaught, she took his place as honorary Colonel of the Grenadier Guards. On her sixteenth birthday, she undertook her first engagement in the role at Windsor Castle where she inspected the Guards alongside her father. It was a great success and afterward she hosted a reception for six hundred officers and men. Yet, the Palace continued to present her as a child.

She was 18 years old in April 1944, the significance of that age in royal terms being that she could now rule in the event of her father's death without requiring a regent. The moment was not marked by any great celebration, but she did move from the nursery into a suite of her own.

Elizabeth's suite boasted upholstery of pink brocade patterned in cream, according to contemporary accounts, and the cream walls were adorned with tranquil pastoral paintings. She had her own armorial bearings and a standard that would be flown in whichever residence she occupied. She was also now permitted her own household, acquiring a lady-in-waiting in July of that year.

As Colonel-in-Chief of the Grenadier Guards, 16-year-old Elizabeth inspects the troops at Windsor Castle in 1942.

A QUIET WORD WITH CHURCHILL

One legal wrangle emerged from Elizabeth's arrival at the age of 18. According to the 1937 Regency Act, she could indeed be Queen at 18 but could not become a Counsellor of State until she was 21. The law, it seemed had been badly drafted and the anomaly was spotted by a lawyer who informed Sir Alexander Hardinge (1894 – 1960), the King's Private Secretary.

Hardinge at first believed it did not matter, that commonsense would prevail. If the Queen could reign, she could surely also be a Counsellor. Not so, argued the Lord Chancellor, Lord Simon (1873 – 1954). But the King intervened at this point, insisting that his daughter had to be a Counsellor of State.

His Majesty had a quiet word with the Prime Minister Winston Churchill, a quick bill was drafted and in July 1944 Princess Elizabeth became a Counsellor along with her mother. The King was away in Italy at the time and, therefore, she performed duties in his place, including giving Royal Assent to Acts passed in Parliament. It is astonishing to think that she was able to do this but was still not old enough to vote in an election of MPs to that same Parliament.

THE MILITARY PRINCESS

Perhaps to mollify the Welsh, the Princess accompanied the King and Queen on a visit to Wales in early 1944. They were greeted by rapturous crowds everywhere they went. People were reported to have walked miles from the villages of south Wales to see the Princess in Cardiff. She was a real symbol of hope for all, not just in Wales but throughout the kingdom.

The young were particularly fascinated by her and everyone wanted to see her. But the Palace still refused to send her out on her own. This began to change in May 1944 when she spoke in public for the very first time at the annual meeting of the Queen Elizabeth Hospital for Children in Hackney in London. In the fall, she launched HMS *Vanguard* in the Clyde shipyards, giving a speech at the ensuing lunch.

It was decided that she would join one of the women's services and in early 1945 the Auxiliary Territorial Service (ATS) was chosen. The royal family had a long naval tradition and it was anticipated that she might join the Women's Royal Naval Service (WRNS). Nonetheless, her parents took a lot of persuading but she finally enlisted as No. 230873 Second Subaltern Elizabeth Alexandra Mary Windsor. It was an honorary rank but she underwent proper training at Aldershot, just like all the other new recruits.

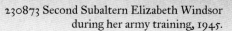

230873 Second Subaltern Elizabeth Windsor during her army training, 1945.

Winston Churchill

Born into an aristocratic family in 1874, his grandfather being John Spencer-Churchill, 7th Duke of Marlborough, Winston Leonard Spencer-Churchill led an extraordinary life and has been acknowledged to be one of the greatest Britons in history. After Harrow School, he enrolled at the Royal Military College, Sandhurst, and enjoyed a brief but eventful career in the British Army. He served on the North-West Frontier and Sudan, where he fought at the Battle of Omdurman in 1898. Meanwhile, he was engaged in journalism, writing military reports for various newspapers, and he also wrote two books detailing his experiences. Leaving the army, he worked as a war correspondent and while reporting on the Boer War, was taken prisoner by the Boers. He escaped, traveling 300 miles to Mozambique and wrote another book about his experiences.

In 1900, he became Conservative MP for Oldham, switching to the Liberal Party four years later. In 1908, having been re-elected, he was appointed President of the Board of Trade. That year he married Clementine Hozier (1885 – 1977). He was First Lord of the Admiralty at the start of the First World War but resigned after the Battle of Gallipoli, having proposed the disastrous expedition. Rejoining the army, he commanded a battalion on the Western Front but returned to government for the final year of the war as Minister of Munitions.

He rejoined the Conservatives in 1922 and, out of government, wrote *A History of English Speaking Peoples*. In the 1930s, he advocated British rearmament against the threat from Nazi Germany and vehemently opposed Prime Minister Neville Chamberlain's policy of appeasement toward Hitler. Following a vote of no confidence in Chamberlain in 1940, Churchill became Prime Minister just hours before Germany launched its Western Offensive.

He became a figurehead for the nation during the war and worked closely with US President Roosevelt and the leader of the USSR, Josef Stalin (1878 – 1953) to finally defeat the Nazis. In the election following the war, however, he was defeated, although he returned to power in 1951. Ill health forced him to resign in 1955 but he remained a Member of Parliament until 1964. He died in 1965 at the age of 90, and received a State Funeral.

NOT THE PRINCESS OF WALES

Around Princess Elizabeth's eighteenth birthday, another debate arose as to whether she should be given the title Princess of Wales. Several Welsh towns petitioned for it and the Welsh Parliamentary Party which was made up of members of the Conservative, Labour, and Liberal parties agreed with them. The Palace was, as ever, reserved on the issue, refusing to bend to populist opinion. The Princess was, after all, merely Heir Presumptive and the title had only ever been given to Heirs Apparent.

The Home Office looked into it and concluded that the sovereign could still have a son which would move Elizabeth back in the succession. Therefore, until she succeeded, she would remain Heir Presumptive. The same had been true of Queen Victoria until she succeeded in 1837. This meant that no woman could ever be Heir Apparent but it did not really deal with the matter of whether Princess Elizabeth could become Princess of Wales. The Garter Principal King of Arms pointed out that if George VI had a son and that son married, there was the unacceptable possibility of there being two women bearing the title Princess of Wales.

Home Secretary, Herbert Morrison (1888 – 1965), insisted that giving Elizabeth the title would please the Welsh and would help to reduce the feeling that the government was somehow anti-Welsh. He added that even if the King had a son the title could simply be allowed to lapse.

The King's wily Private Secretary received Morrison's note but withheld it from the King. It mattered little because George was against the idea from the beginning. He told Winston Churchill to ensure that the story was killed off in the press and the Palace announced that there would be no change in the Princess's title on her birthday. Wales would not have a Prince of Wales until 1958 when Prince Charles took the title.

Princess Elizabeth at age 18 in 1944.

Sir Alan "Tommy" Lascelles

British courtier, Sir Alan Frederick "Tommy" Lascelles (1887 – 1981) was private secretary to both King George VI and to Queen Elizabeth II. The son of Commander Frederick Canning Lascelles and Frederica Maria Liddell, he was a cousin of Henry Lascelles, 6th Earl of Harewood who married Mary, the Princess Royal who was the daughter of King George V and Queen Mary. Lascelles went to Marlborough School and then studied at Trinity College, Oxford. He served with the Bedfordshire Yeomanry during the First World War and from 1919 to 1920 was aide-de-camp to his brother-in-law, Lord Lloyd (1879 – 1941), the Governor of Bombay.

Back in England, Lascelles became Assistant Private Secretary to Edward when he was Prince of Wales, a position he held until 1929 when he resigned due to disagreements with the Prince. He was appointed Secretary to the Governor General of Canada, a position he held from 1931 to 1935.

In 1936, after the abdication of Edward VIII, Lascelles was named private secretary to King George VI and in 1939, he was knighted by the King on board a train during the monarch's hugely successful tour of the United States and Canada, a tour that Lascelles had played a large part in organizing. He was Private Secretary to the Queen from 1952 to 1953. He died in 1981, at age 94.

JUST AN ORDINARY SOLDIER

Orders went out that she was to be treated no differently to any other officer undergoing the same training and the Queen ensured that there were no facilities for photographers. However, this did not prevent the press from taking more pictures of the Princess than possibly at any other time in her life so far.

Magazines and newspapers around the Allied world were full of snaps of her in uniform, holding a spanner or leaning on the hood of an army vehicle. It proved hard, therefore, for her to be just an ordinary soldier. Furthermore, she was not allowed to mix very much with her colleagues. But she acquired a rudimentary knowledge of driving, engines, and car maintenance.

She would later say that this was the only time in her life when she could truly measure her own capabilities against those of others of her age. The training lasted six weeks after which she was a qualified driver. At the end of July, just before the end of the war, she was promoted to Junior Commander.

ROYAL ENTERTAINMENTS

During the war the Princesses staged a series of entertainments—Christmas shows—that were performed before their parents and others who lived and worked at Windsor Castle. The first was in 1940 when they successfully performed a play called "The Christmas Child." It was staged in St. George's Hall and the 14-year-old Princess Elizabeth took the part of one of the three kings. The other two were played by boys who had been evacuated from London.

At Christmas 1941 they put on a pantomime, "Cinderella," that had been written especially for them by a local schoolmaster. Again, it was a success. In 1942 they performed in "Sleeping Beauty" in which the future Queen memorably took the arms of two boys in the roles of sailors and sang a song entitled "Mind Your Sisters."

As the years passed, the stage sets and costumes became increasingly ambitious but one constant was that the Princesses had lead roles. Attention was always focused upon them, regardless of the competencies of the local children and evacuees who also took part. Audiences increased, and locally-based soldiers and ATS women came to watch.

They did one performance in 1943 specifically for the troops. The press reviewed them and of Princess Elizabeth's performance as Aladdin in the 1943 pantomime, one critic said:

> *From the moment Princess Elizabeth popped out of a laundry basket, the King and Queen and the audience of 400 laughed and thoroughly enjoyed the show.*

Even Sir Alan Lascelles was impressed and wrote in his diary that the show would not have disgraced Drury Lane. The last pantomime was staged at Christmas 1944 and in it the heir to the throne could be seen as a Victorian seaside belle.

Princess Margaret (left) and Princess Elizabeth in the play Aladdin, 1943.

PART TWO

THE EYES
OF THE NATION

As long as we live, it will be the constant purpose of Lieutenant Mountbatten and myself to serve a people who are so dear to me and to show ourselves deserving of their esteem.

Princess Elizabeth on her engagement in 1947

CHAPTER 6

RUMORS OF A ROYAL ROMANCE

VICTORY IN EUROPE

The end of the Second World War signaled an outbreak of partying in the United Kingdom. Whether it was relief at the realization that they had survived or the knowledge that evil had been defeated, the people of Britain celebrated joyously and the King, Queen, and their two daughters were placed firmly at the fulcrum of the celebrations.

VE Day (Victory in Europe Day) was on May 8, 1945, but celebrations went on for three days. It was estimated that the crowds around the Queen Victoria Memorial in front of Buckingham Palace on the afternoon of that momentous day were even greater than those that had gathered after the King's Coronation.

Women wore red, white, and blue rosettes with ribbons in their hair and Winston Churchill drove through the crowd, stopping along the way to make spontaneous speeches. He went into the palace and had lunch with King George and Queen Elizabeth. A little later the crowd began chanting "We want the King! We want the King!"

The King obliged them by appearing on the balcony, accompanied by his wife and the two Princesses. "For he's a jolly good fellow" rang out from below. Churchill then appeared alongside them on the balcony flashing his "V for victory" sign with his fingers. Later that evening the royal family would again respond to the chants of the crowd and reappeared on the balcony.

GOING OUT ON THE TOWN

A group of Guards officers—friends of the Princesses—joined the royal family at dinner that evening but after the meal Princess Margaret came up with the idea of going out into the crowd. Amazingly, the King and Queen gave their permission and accompanied by a police sergeant, the Princesses and the Guards exited the palace surreptitiously. They walked, unrecognized on St. James's Street and along Piccadilly.

They all wore military uniforms, apart from Princess Margaret, and blended in with all the other similarly clad people. It must have been a peculiar feeling for the two girls, walking freely in the streets, mixing with the crowd, something they had never in their lives been allowed to do.

Later Elizabeth recalled the fear of being recognized "... I pulled my uniform cap down over my eyes," and the euphoria "... lines of people linking arms and walking down Whitehall, and all of us were swept along by tides of happiness and relief."

Returning to the palace, they stood at the railings, orchestrating new chants of "We want the King!" One of them went into the palace and persuaded the monarch out onto the balcony, his daughters cheering with everyone else down below.

CHURCHILL LEAVES OFFICE

VJ Day (Victory over Japan Day) followed the same pattern on August 15. But there was now a new Prime Minister. The General Election of

1945 had ousted the Conservative government and Winston Churchill left office.

Instead the Labour Party's Clement Attlee (1883 – 1967) now occupied 10 Downing Street. Attlee was an altogether different type of man to Churchill. His rhetoric recognized the need to celebrate but emphasized also the necessity of getting back to work. "We are right to rejoice at the victory of the people," he proclaimed from the balcony of the Ministry of Health, "and it is right for a short time that we should relax. But I want to remind you that we have a great deal of work to do to win the peace as we won the war."

A recorded speech by the King was broadcast through speakers and the royal family made more appearances on the balcony of Buckingham Palace. Again, the Princesses took to the streets that night but this time they were recognized and surrounded by cheering subjects. The police intervened and the girls were allowed to go off and enjoy themselves.

MELTING CLEMENT ATTLEE

Life slowly returned to normal after the royal family had been reunited in the early months of 1945. In August, Princess Elizabeth was taken to Ascot Racecourse to watch champion jockey Gordon Richards win five races. That day at lunch the King was informed by US President Truman (1884 – 1972) that an atom bomb had been dropped on Hiroshima.

Most of the time though, the King was busy bolstering morale in war-ravaged Britain. He was unhappy that Winston Churchill had been voted out of office, partly because of what they had gone through together, but also because he feared the social reform and the nationalization program Clement Attlee had campaigned on. His private politics were to the right and the Queen's were even more so.

He need not have been discomfited because Attlee bent over backward to keep him onside. For instance, when the King expressed disquiet at the prospect of Hugh Dalton (1887 – 1962), Member of Parliament for Bishop Auckland, and rebellious son of George V's tutor, Canon John Neale Dalton (1839 – 1931), becoming Foreign Secretary, Attlee immediately acquiesced and moved Dalton to the Treasury.

In fact, the King had little to worry about. There was not a whiff of republicanism in this post-war Labour government and the King and the socialists worked well together. The Queen described the new Prime Minister as "a practical little man … quite cagey … difficult to get along with, but he soon melted."

The King and Queen with Princess Elizabeth, Princess Margaret, and Winston Churchill on the balcony of Buckingham Palace on VE Day, May 8, 1945.

Clement Attlee

Clement Richard Attlee (1883 – 1967) was leader of the Labour Party from 1935 to 1955. He served as prime minister from 1945 to 1951, a critical time in British history as the government attempted to rebuild a country effectively rendered bankrupt by the Second World War.

Attlee was born into a middle-class family in London and trained as a lawyer after graduating from Oxford University. Deeply affected by the poverty he saw in London's East End, he joined the Independent Labour Party in 1908. After the First World War, in which he achieved the rank of major, he went into politics, becoming Member of Parliament for Limehouse, east London, in 1922.

From 1942 until 1945, during the Second World War, he was Deputy Prime Minister to Winston Churchill in the wartime coalition government. When a general election was called at the end of the war he won a surprising landslide victory over the great war leader.

His premiership was a period of intense activity. His government enlarged and improved social services, creating the National Health Service with care provided for British citizens "from cradle to grave." Major industries and public utilities such as coal mining, electricity, and the railways were brought under state control and his government presided over the decolonization of India, Pakistan, Ceylon, and Jordan. The state of Israel was created when Britain withdrew from Palestine.

In the general election of 1950, Labour lost its large majority and by the time of the 1951 election, it was time for change. Churchill returned to 10 Downing Street while Attlee stayed on as leader of the Labour Party for a further four years.

Clement Attlee died in 1967 at the age of 84. He is often reckoned in surveys by academics to have been the most successful British prime minister in history.

FLYING SOLO

Elizabeth was busier now, undertaking more solo engagements. Her future as Queen was now looking increasingly certain and her duties reflected the priorities of both the palace and the government. Thus, in the summer of 1945 she opened a new library at the Royal College of Nursing, presented prizes to students at the Royal Free School of Medicine for Women, inspected the Fifth Battalion and Training Battalion of the Grenadier Guards and addressed an assembly of 3,000 Welsh Girl Guides.

When the King and Queen visited Northern Ireland, she was with them. It was her first flight, a short hop from Northolt aerodrome to Long Kesh. She returned to Northern Ireland in 1946 on her own. The objective of the trip was to support the Union. It was a Protestant tour and the places that she visited and the people she met underscored this. By this time, the King was beginning to be affected by arteriosclerosis, often suffering considerable pain in his legs.

A QUESTION OF MARRIAGE

Unlike most other girls her age, Princess Elizabeth had not gone through the rituals of falling in and out of love or enjoying the heartache of teenage crushes. But there was one young man for whom she seems to have had feelings from her early teens. A courtier said "There really was no one else she could possibly marry but Prince Philip." Unlike many of her forebears, the decision as to who she was going to marry lay in her hands and not in the control of her parents or the palace.

Philip had a lot going for him. He was a prince and, therefore, royal and he was a pleasant and good-looking young man. He had been known to the royal family since he was very young and Princess Elizabeth knew him well, having been with him at several family gatherings before the war. He had been at the 1934 wedding of the Duke and Duchess of Kent and had attended the Coronation in 1937.

When potential bridegrooms for the Princess were considered by the newspapers, his name was often listed. The first time the two met seriously was at a tea party on the royal yacht *Victoria and Albert*. This meeting had been contrived by Prince Philip's uncle, Lord Louis Mountbatten (1900 – 79) who wrote: "Philip came back aboard *V&A* for tea and was a great success with the children."

ROYAL REFUGEES

Philip seemed an ideal choice as suitor for the young Princess. He was royal and, in fact, could be said to be even more royal than Elizabeth was. Both his mother and his father were from royal families, whereas only Elizabeth's father was royal. He had also been born into a reigning royal family and was the grandson and nephew of Kings of Greece. The present circumstances of his family were not entirely auspicious, however. They could be said, after all, to be refugees, having fled Greece.

It had been a British warship that had helped them escape, something for which Princess Alice, Philip's mother, was eternally grateful to King George V. They went into exile, dispossessed, stateless, and impoverished. There were those who insisted that Philip was not really Greek, emphasizing his Danish blood.

Philip also had connections to Germany through his four sisters, all now German through marriage. His family life had been unstable and possibly quite disturbing. His mother was not only mentally ill, she was also deaf. She once said that she was only able to communicate with her children when they were old enough to speak and she could lip-read.

But, undoubtedly, his nomadic lifestyle, shunting from one family member to another, taught him to live by his wits. He was seen by his cousin Alexandra, Queen of Yugoslavia, as "a huge hungry dog, perhaps a friendly collie who had never had a basket of his own." The death in 1938 of the 2nd Marquess of Milford Haven left him, as one commentator has put it "stateless, nameless and not far from penniless."

Lord Louis Mountbatten

Louis Francis Albert Victor Nicholas Mountbatten, 1st Earl Mountbatten of Burma (1900 – 79) was born Prince Louis of Battenberg at Windsor, England. His father, also named Prince Louis of Battenberg (1854 – 1921), became the 1st Marquess of Milford Haven in 1917, renouncing his family's German titles and changing the family name to Mountbatten. He was an officer in the Royal Navy who was related to the British royal family. Lord Mountbatten's mother was Princess Victoria of Hesse and by Rhine (1863 – 1950). He was a great-grandson of Queen Victoria and Prince Philip's mother, Princess Alice, was his sister.

During the First World War Mountbatten was in the Royal Navy and in the Second World War, he commanded the 5th Destroyer Flotilla aboard the destroyer HMS *Kelly* which was sunk by German dive-bombers during the Battle of Crete. The incident was used by Noël Coward (1899 – 1973) in his 1942 patriotic war film *In Which We Serve*. Mountbatten was appointed Chief of Combined Operations. Under his command, the ill-conceived and ultimately disastrous Dieppe Raid of August 1942 was undertaken. In October 1943, he was promoted to Supreme Allied Commander, South East Asia Command and under his command, Burma was re-taken. In 1945, he received the formal surrender of Japanese forces in Singapore. He ended the war with the naval rank of Rear-Admiral.

In 1947, Mountbatten was given the role of overseeing the transition of British India to independence. The aim was to create a united India, but in August 1947, the country split into India and Pakistan. Thereafter, he returned to the Royal Navy and, forty years after his father held the same rank, he was appointed First Sea Lord. In 1959, he became Chief of the Defence Staff, in which role he was head of the British Armed Forces. He became extremely close—and something of a mentor—to his grand-nephew Prince Charles who called him "Honorary Grandfather."

On August 27, 1979, Mountbatten was assassinated along with his grandson Nicholas, and two others by the Provisional Irish Republican Army (IRA), which had placed a bomb in his fishing boat, *Shadow V*, in Mullaghmore, County Sligo, Ireland.

Prince Philip, Duke of Edinburgh

Prince Philip (born 1921) was a member of the House of Schleswig-Holstein-Sonderburg-Glücksburg, and was born on the Greek island of Corfu into the Greek and Danish royal families. He was the only son, but fifth child of Prince Andrew of Greece and Denmark (1882 – 1944) and Princess Alice of Battenberg (1885 – 1969). In 1922 when Philip's uncle, King Constantine I of Greece (1868 – 1923) was forced to abdicate, Philip's father was exiled from Greece for life.

The family settled in Paris where Philip was educated before being sent to England to attend Cheam School, living with his maternal grandmother, Victoria Mountbatten, Dowager Marchioness of Milford Haven (1863 – 1950) at Kensington Palace and his uncle George Mountbatten, 2nd Marquess of Milford Haven (1892 – 1938) in Bray in Berkshire. Life for his family was changing. His four sisters married German aristocrats and moved to Germany, his mother was diagnosed with schizophrenia and his father moved into a small apartment in Monaco.

In 1933, he was sent to Schule Schloss Salem in Germany which was owned by the family of his brother-in-law, Berthold, Margrave of Baden (1906 – 63). As Nazism came to the fore in Germany, the school's Jewish founder, Kurt Hahn (1886 – 1974), fled to Britain and founded Gordonstoun School in Moray in Scotland. Philip moved to Scotland to attend Gordonstoun, leaving in 1939 to join the Royal Navy.

He graduated the following year from the Royal Naval College at Dartmouth as the best cadet on his course. He served with distinction during the Second World War and among many actions, was involved in the Battle of Crete and was mentioned in dispatches during the Battle of Cape Matapan. He ended the war as a lieutenant.

In 1939, when Princess Elizabeth was 13 years old, Prince Philip escorted her and her sister around the Naval College during a visit with her parents. They were his third cousins through Queen Victoria and second cousins twice removed through King Christian IX of Denmark.

They began writing to each other shortly afterward and in 1946, he asked King George VI for his daughter's hand in marriage. The engagement was announced on July 10, 1947, and they were married on November 20 of the same year.

PHILIP'S INTENTIONS BECOME CLEAR

As the war progressed, Philip continued writing letters to Elizabeth and in 1943 he received an invitation to spend Christmas with the royal family at Windsor Castle. It was an invitation he hastily accepted.

Philip attended that year's Christmas entertainment and apparently entered fully into the spirit of the occasion. He and the new young 3rd Marquess of Milford Haven (1919 – 70) enjoyed a family dinner with the royals and they partied until one in the morning. It was the moment, Crawfie later explained, that things changed between Elizabeth and the dashing young navy officer. She was delighted to finally be like other girls her age, having a young serviceman fighting for his country to whom she could write letters.

Naturally, the press picked up on his visit and the rumor mill went into overdrive. The Greek royal family, exiled in Egypt, began to take an interest. In fact, it has been said that not long after the Windsor party, Philip had declared to the Greek King his intentions regarding the Princess. Sir Alan Lascelles recorded in his diary on April 2, 1944, that Prince Philip had discussed his suitability for marriage to the Princess with his uncle and King George VI but that the idea had been rejected.

Lord Mountbatten continued to scheme behind the scenes, however, and the next stage of his plan was for Philip to be granted British citizenship. Meanwhile, Philip and Elizabeth met in various places such as Coppins in Buckinghamshire, where the Duke of Kent and his family lived, and at Buckingham Palace. The King finally took an interest in Philip's naturalization, enquiring of the Home Office what needed to be done.

HOT GOSSIP AND TENDER SMILES

By October 1945 Philip had become a parliamentary issue. The government were concerned that supporting him might be interpreted as support for the royalists in Greece. The government had to consider very carefully its diplomatic efforts in the Balkans. Prime Minister Attlee proposed leaving it on the table until after Greece had held elections and a plebiscite, due the following year.

Philip returned to Britain in early 1946, working at the naval training establishment in North Wales. He traveled frequently to Buckingam Palace and Crawfie noticed the difference he brought to the young Princess. She now seemed to be taking more care over her appearance and her governess recalls the incessant playing of the gramophone recording of "People Will Say We're in Love," one of the tunes from the hit musical *Oklahoma*.

Philip attended the second marriage of his sister Princess Sophie (1914 – 2001) at Salem in Baden. He had not seen Sophie since before the start of the war and she had remained in Germany throughout, losing her first husband in the fighting. She recalled Philip telling her that he was considering getting engaged and that "Uncle Dickie [Lord Mountbatten] was being very helpful."

Philip and Elizabeth attended many of the same parties, but with the air thick with hot gossip, they were careful not to be seen dancing together. Gradually, stories about the couple published in foreign newspapers began to appear in the popular press in Britain. Palace denials ensued but did little to crush the rumors, especially when Elizabeth was caught on a newsreel film attending a wedding and smiling tenderly in Philip's direction.

THE UNPOLISHED PRINCE

The Greeks voted in September 1946 to restore the monarchy, but George II's record of authoritarian rule in Greece was not encouraging to the British government. Around this time, Philip was informed that his leave to remain in the Royal Navy depended on whether he was allowed to become a British citizen.

But things were moving far too slowly for Lord Mountbatten and he began to vigorously lobby the Palace. Sir Alan Lascelles was particularly irritated by the numerous phone calls on the matter he was receiving. Eventually, the Home Secretary and Attlee agreed to the naturalization of Prince Philip and he adopted his Uncle Louis' name, Mountbatten, as his surname.

It was still a delicate matter, however, and many Labour backbenchers felt uneasy at Philip's connection to a disagreeable Greek dynasty. There was also concern that the Prince was being shown favoritism at a time when many foreigners, displaced by the war, were attempting to become British citizens.

Lord Mountbatten launched a charm offensive in response to persuade the press that Philip was, to all intents and purposes, already British. It was emphasized that Philip had nothing to do with Greek politics and, in fact, had spent no more than three months in the country since he had been one year old. Furthermore, he could not speak Greek and his wish to be British, it was said, dated back to the time before the rumors of the royal engagement had started.

THE KING'S CONSTANT COMPANION

There may have been several reasons for the Palace dragging its heels somewhat on the matter of Prince Philip's naturalization and some of them may have been partly to do with the fact that Lord Mountbatten wanted it so much. Mountbatten and the King were close, but Mountbatten's political machinations and love of intrigue, plus his closeness to the Labour government did not entirely endear him to the sovereign.

Mountbatten was unfailingly ambitious and if the Palace gave in to him on this matter it would look like they were bending to his indomitable will. The Palace were also worried that Prince Philip might act as a Trojan horse for his Uncle Dickie, allowing him to introduce reforming ideas that would change the monarchy forever.

Undoubtedly though, the King was also reluctant to lose his elder daughter. She had acted, in the words of Lady Airlie, as "his constant companion in shooting, walking, riding—in fact in everything," and he was afraid of that being taken away. Her parents may also have simply considered the Princess too young and lacking in experience to marry. Philip was, after all the first young man she had really met.

TOO FORTHRIGHT BY FAR

Philip seemed to be one of those individuals that people either loved or hated. He was full of life, was honest, and a born leader and it was for those reasons that he had found success at naval college and then later during his naval service. These attributes also endeared him to the fairer sex.

He was too honest and forthright by far, some would have said, especially the older generation, and was abrupt and intolerant of stuffiness. These qualities did not go down well at court and among the aristocracy, chained as it was to ritual and tradition. One courtier went as far as to say that the King and Queen considered him "rough, ill-tempered, and uneducated." They also questioned whether he would remain faithful to his wife. "Unpolished" was the polite description used for him by some guests of the King and Queen at Balmoral.

Philip's German connections did not help. But this was fairly ridiculous, given the royal family's own close ties to Germany over the past two hundred years. The Queen's brother, David Bowes-Lyon advised her against the union and one Conservative lord nicknamed Philip "Charlie Kraut." The antipathy to Philip was noted by Princess Elizabeth's private secretary Jock Colville (1915 – 87) in his diary:

> *Lords Salisbury (1893 – 1972), Eldon (1899 – 1976) and Stanley (1865 – 1948) think him no gentleman, and in a sense they are right. They also profess to see in him a Teutonic strain.*

Schooling was another cause of the snobbery expressed about the Prince. He had not gone to the "right schools" which probably meant Eton. Instead, he had gone to Gordonstoun which, in the elite's eyes, made him a socialist. Thus, he did not have the appropriate connections, the kind that Eton creates so well.

One member of the royal family expressed the feelings of many in the elite about Philip's education, that he "had been to a crank school with theories of complete social equality where the boys were taught to mix with all and sundry."

It would take Prince Philip many years to achieve acceptance by the courtly and aristocratic world that he was entering.

Princess Elizabeth and Prince Philip act as bridesmaid and usher at the wedding of Patricia Mountbatten and Lord Brabourne in London, October 26, 1946.

WOMAN OF THE WEEK

Elizabeth was oblivious to all the whispering. She wanted to marry Philip and it seemed the British public wanted the same thing. Many thought that he was ideal for the role of consort, a job that was little more than ceremonial.

All the time, Elizabeth was becoming more visible to the public, with photographs of her in all the magazines alongside hints about the putative romance. In January 1947, she was voted one of the most glamorous women in the world by the International Artists' Committee in New York.

Two months later *Time* magazine named her as their "Woman of the Week," describing her as practical, down-to-earth and human. The four-page spread on her life described her pastime of riding and said that she was an enthusiastic dancer, a lover of swing music, and a young woman who liked to get her own way in things. She was said to enjoy knitting, reading bestsellers, and gossiping with her sister and friends over tea in front of a fire at Buckingham Palace.

She certainly enjoyed the musicals that came to the London stage and Jean Woodroffe (born 1923), who would later become a lady-in-waiting to her, fondly remembers she and the Princess singing the hit songs of the day during long car journeys. There were madrigal singing sessions at the palace at which either Margaret or a professional pianist played and the sisters sang, often with the accompaniment of some army officers.

DRESSING FOR DINNER

One of those officers was Lord Porchester (1924 – 2001), known to the Princess as "Porchey." His father, Lord Carnarvon, had been a leading racehorse owner-breeder at the beginning of the twentieth century and had established the Highclere Stud at his home of Highclere Castle. Porchey became the Princess's escort to the races and became her racing manager when she was Queen.

Princess Elizabeth's sporting interests were just one example of how different she was to her sister Princess Margaret. As they grew older, and as Prince Philip appeared on the scene, this was even more the case. Elizabeth's circle of friends seemed altogether more staid than the

wilder set with whom Margaret increasingly ran about.

It has to be remembered that this was a time in royal circles when one had to change clothing twice in the evening, once for high-tea and then for dinner. Margaret enjoyed being amused, having fun, in a way that Elizabeth did not, or perhaps could not. She was an introvert while her sister was an extrovert, always on the lookout for fun.

Margaret enjoyed people while Elizabeth seemed to hold back, not able to give herself entirely to the company in which she found herself. In the mid-1940s, she was still remembered as quiet and rather shy. Jock Colville noted that:

[she] has the sweetest of characters, but she is not easy to talk to, except when one sits next to her at dinner, and her worth, which I take to be very real, is not on the surface.

THE ROYAL STUD

Lord Porchester was as passionate about horses as the Princess. The two had often met during the war at the Beckhampton stables in Wiltshire. It was there that horses bred at the royal studs were trained. Horses became for Elizabeth, her real escape from the rigors and strictures of royal duty. She read voraciously about them and developed an excellent knowledge of equine management.

The royal studs had been established in the sixteenth century at Hampton Court but were later moved to Windsor. While still Prince of Wales, Edward VII created the Sandringham stud in the late nineteenth century. Royal managers became obsessed with bloodlines, even those of horses' owners and if the owner was not suitable, the royal mare was unlikely to be covered by his stallion. On one occasion, Captain Charles Moore, George VI's and later Queen Elizabeth's manager, rejected a stallion because its owner happened to be a bookmaker.

Lord Porchester had studied at Cirencester Agricultural College and attempted to change royal habits regarding the social status of a horse's owners. He and Princess Elizabeth worked together and later as Queen, Elizabeth would take an even greater interest in horse breeding. In 1962, she took out a lease on Polhampton Lodge Stud, near Overton in Hampshire, to concentrate on the breeding of racehorses. She worked ever more closely with Porchey, especially after he took over as her racing manager. One royal confidante said: "Henry tells her a lot of gossip. She's very fond of him and he's devoted to her."

THE GREAT IMPERIAL MISSION

The royal family's first overseas trip together was to the British colonies of South Africa and Rhodesia. They were to spend three months there and added to that was the month on board HMS *Vanguard* getting there and back. They embarked on February 1, 1947. The trip was important on several levels, described by Sir John Wheeler-Bennett (1902 – 75), biographer of George VI, as a "great imperial mission."

Firstly, it was hoped that the visit of the royal family would save the government of Jan Smuts (1870 – 1950) and protect the British Crown in South Africa. English-speaking South Africans were enthusiastic about the visit, Afrikaners less so. George VI was to them a symbol of the British Empire and they wanted to break away from the imperial shackles.

The second aspect of the "imperial mission" however, although incidental, exercised the press and broadcasters. Princess Elizabeth and Prince Philip would be separated for four months. It has been suggested that the tour was an effort by the King to disentangle the pair but this seems unlikely, given that it had been arranged so long in advance.

Some had expected the engagement to be announced before the tour and when this failed to happen, speculation only became greater. Perhaps all was not going well between them, some suggested. Perhaps, as a former courtier later said, the King and Queen saw the trip as something of a cooling-off period for the couple.

CROSSING THE EQUATOR

The journey on HMS *Vanguard* was pretty rough and the royal party were mainly confined to their cabins with sea-sickness. Nonetheless, there was some fun to be had with activities such as the crossing-the-line ceremony when they passed the Equator. The weather, too, was better than back home where the worst weather of the century was being endured.

It was the first time the Princesses had set foot outside the United Kingdom and they

Princess Elizabeth playing tag with midshipmen while on board HMS *Vanguard*.

Sir John "Jock" Colville

Sir John "Jock" Colville (1915 – 87) was the son of the Hon. George Colville, secretary of the Institute of Chartered Accountants. His father was the younger son of Charles Colville, 1st Viscount of Culross (1818 – 1903) who was Tory Chief Whip and also served the royal household as Master of the Buckhounds, an officer in the Master of the Horse's department. Jock Colville's mother, Lady Cynthia was a courtier and social worker.

Colville was a Page of Honor from 1927 to 1931, a position he gained through his mother's work as an attendant to the Queen. But his mother also ensured that she took him with her to the child welfare center she ran in the poor district of Shoreditch in London.

He attended West Downs School in Winchester before going to Harrow and Trinity College, Cambridge. He became private secretary to three prime ministers—Neville Chamberlain, Winston Churchill, and Clement Attlee and was private secretary to Princess Elizabeth from 1947 to 1949.

He is perhaps best known for the diaries he kept, especially prized for his observations of Winston Churchill's premierships.

Henry Herbert, 7th Earl of Carnarvon

The 7th Earl of Carnarvon (1924 – 2001), styled Lord Porchester, was the son of the 6th Earl of Carnarvon and his American-born wife Catherine Wendell, and the grandson of the 5th Earl (1866 – 1923) who was the financial backer of the search for and excavation of the tomb of Tutankhamun in Egypt's Valley of the Kings. He died of blood poisoning caused by an infected mosquito bite in 1923, his death leading to rumors of the "Curse of Tutankhamun" or the "Mummy's Curse."

Lord Porchester served as a lieutenant in the Royal Horse Guards and was later appointed Honorary Colonel of the 116th Engineer Regiment of the Territorial Army. He was famously, a close friend of Queen Elizabeth II and became manager of her racing stables in 1969, retaining the position until his death. He was invested as a Knight Commander of the Royal Victorian order (KCVO) in 1982 and died in 2001.

Sir John "Jock" Coville.

The Queen and Lord Porchester watch the exciting finish of the 1978 Epsom Derby.

were extremely excited. For Elizabeth, duty always called and the visit must have brought home to her the responsibilities for the affairs of the British Commonwealth that lay ahead.

They arrived in Cape Town on February 17, where they were welcomed enthusiastically by a large crowd, allaying fears of Republican protest. That first night they enjoyed a state banquet, described by Sir Alan Lascelles as the dreariest dinner he had been at in thirty years of similar functions. But he did record that the royal family was happy enough. "Princess Elizabeth is delightfully enthusiastic and interested," he wrote.

SOUTH AFRICAN CELEBRATIONS

They were to visit every part of the Union of South Africa and traveled in a special "White Train" that was their home for thirty-five nights. Their travels took in the Orange Free State, Basutoland, Natal, and the Transvaal

before moving on to Northern Rhodesia and Bechuanaland. The visit was diverse as South Africa did not yet have the apartheid laws that were to cause so much controversy in the coming decades.

The Princesses did not really have much to do apart from accompanying their parents to functions and events. Princess Elizabeth's twenty-first birthday fell three days before the end of the tour. Back home in Britain the newspapers all carried profiles of her, but South Africa pushed the boat out with extravagant celebrations. The day was declared a public holiday and there was a large ceremony at which the Princess reviewed the South African armed forces.

A WHOLE EMPIRE IS LISTENING

Elizabeth gave a speech at a youth rally that included all races and colors of the Union, attended a reception at Cape Town's City Hall, and a ball in her honor where Jan Smuts

Princess Elizabeth and Princess Margaret followed by the Queen, at the Kenilworth racecourse, Cape Town, during their tour of South Africa, 1947.

presented her with the gift of a necklace of twenty-one gemstones as well as a gold key to the city.

That same day she also broadcast to the Empire and Commonwealth a speech written by Sir Alan Lascelles. It would become one of the most celebrated orations of her life. In fact, she later said that when she had looked at an early draft, the speech had made her cry. In it she famously committed herself to serving her people wherever they may be:

> *There is a motto which has been borne by many of my ancestors—a noble motto, "I serve." Those words were an inspiration to many bygone heirs to the Throne when they made their knightly dedication as they came to manhood. I cannot do quite as they did. But through the inventions of science I can do what was not possible for any of them. I can make my solemn act of dedication with a whole Empire listening. I should like to make that dedication now. It is very simple. I declare before you all that my whole life whether it be long or short shall be devoted to your service and the service of our great imperial family to which we all belong. But I shall not have strength to carry out this resolution alone unless you join in it with me, as I now invite you to do: I know that your support will be unfailingly given. God help me to make good my vow, and God bless all of you who are willing to share in it.*

A FORMIDABLE FORCE EMERGES

The South African tour had had a number of important objectives and it had achieved them. Smuts had been supported against the Afrikaner threat; and the British people, still suffering under restrictions and austerity caused by the war, were reassured that the Empire was still alive and well. It had also emphasized the importance of the Monarchy as the link that tied a diverse group of nations together across the world. Importantly, however, it also

marked the emergence of Princess Elizabeth as a formidable royal force.

Ultimately, Smuts and the Crown in South Africa were doomed to failure. Smuts was voted out of government in the 1948 general election, replaced by a new pro-apartheid government. South Africa finally left the Commonwealth in 1961.

Princess Elizabeth broadcasts from the gardens of Government House in Cape Town, South Africa, on the occasion of her 21st birthday, April 21, 1947.

CHAPTER 8

ANNOUNCING THE BETROTHAL

Engagement

It is with the greatest pleasure that the King and Queen announce the betrothal of their dearly beloved daughter, the Princess Elizabeth, to Lt. Philip Mountbatten, RN, son of the late Prince Andrew of Greece and Princess Andrew (Princess Alice of Battenburg) to which union the King has gladly given his consent.

The life of Prince Philip changed forever following the announcement of his engagement to Princess Elizabeth. He gained a valet and was assigned a detective but he also became a public figure. Even his car became famous, a black MG sports car with the number plate HDK 99. In fact, a letter written by the Princess to Betty Shew who was writing a book to mark the forthcoming royal wedding recalls an early encounter with the paparazzi:

Philip enjoys driving and does it fast! He has his own tiny MG which he is very proud of— he has taken me about in it, once up to London, which was great fun, only it was like sitting on the road, and the wheels are almost as high as one's head. On that one and only occasion we were chased by a photographer which was disappointing.

THE WARDROBE OF A BANK CLERK

Philip carried on working, however, living on his pay as a lieutenant with a wardrobe reported by his new valet to be "scantier than that of many a bank clerk." The newspapers took delight in presenting him as impoverished, and Lady Airlie was surprised by his appearance, describing him as having "the usual after-the-war-look." The retainers at Buckingham Palace were aghast when he began arriving without a hat and wearing an open-necked shirt with rolled up sleeves.

The match had to receive formal approval under the 1772 Royal Marriages Act from not just His Majesty, but also the Privy Council. This having been granted in August, Prince Philip joined the royal family at Balmoral. The guests included Lord and Lady Eldon (1913 – 69), Lord and Lady Salisbury (1897 – 1982), the Duke of Kent, David Bowes-Lyon, and the publisher and later Conservative politician Mark Bonham-Carter (1922 – 94), several of whom disapproved of Prince Philip.

The date was set for November 20, 1947, but before that the Princess was busy, having replaced the Duke of Gloucester as stand-in for the King at functions and ceremonies. She also took part alongside her father in her first state opening of Parliament. Accompanied by a lady-in-waiting, she rode to the Palace of Westminster in the fabulous glass coach, huge crowds lining the route between the two palaces just to catch a glimpse of the soon-to-be-married Elizabeth.

AN ABBEY WEDDING

These days we are used to elaborate royal weddings, the event being broadcast on television to hundreds of millions around the world. In the nineteenth and early twentieth century, royal weddings were fairly private, involving mainly the family itself. The wedding of George VI and Elizabeth Bowes-Lyon at Westminster Abbey was an exception to this general rule.

Thus the decision to hold Elizabeth's wedding at the Abbey turned it into something of a sensation. Historical lows in British history have always been punctuated by royal celebrations to lift the mood of the people, and this would be just such an occasion that the whole country could celebrate. It would be the type of party not seen in Britain since the end of the war and before that, the day of the King's own Coronation.

The royal marriage would also be a cosmopolitan occasion. The British Commonwealth would be on show for the rest of the world to admire. Moreover, it was hoped that a glamorous wedding ceremony would finally bury the memory of the last royal marriage, that of the disgraced Edward VIII and Mrs. Simpson.

But it was still a time of austerity. A fuel shortage had closed factories and the huge loan that the United States had given to help in post-war reconstruction had run out. An emergency budget was set for November to try to deal with Britain's appalling financial plight. It would mean a serious tightening of belts.

Against such a background, there was understandable disquiet about the cost of the royal wedding. The response from the government was that the only element for the day funded by the taxpayer would be the decorations in Whitehall and around Buckingham Palace. Everything else would be paid for from the King's Civil List.

A BAD TIME FOR A PAY RISE

The marriage of the heir to the throne meant a change in Elizabeth's circumstances but given the country's economic situation it was a bad time for a pay rise. Nonetheless, the Palace requested that the Princess's Civil List allowance be increased. It had already been automatically increased from £6,000 a year to £15,000 when she had reached 21. Now the Palace requested that it be raised to £50,000 a year for her and her husband.

Princess Elizabeth and Prince Philip when they announced their engagement, 1947.

It was a political impossibility for the government to agree this amount. Matters were not helped by the fact that the Chancellor of the Exchequer was none other than the Royal family's bête noire, the anti-monarchist Hugh Dalton. The matter was solved at a meeting between Prime Minister Attlee, Dalton, Sir Alan Lascelles, and Sir Ulick Alexander (1889 – 1973), Keeper of the Privy Purse. There was a fear that a Select Committee might have to be set up to look into royal finances, something neither party wanted.

In the meeting, however, Dalton brought up the £200,000 that the King had loaned the government out of a surplus in the Royal Household Balances during the war. Dalton met the King to discuss this matter on October 27. It seemed to go well, but there remained issues to be settled. How much, for instance were the royal couple to be paid. They also had to establish the status of the loan. The government evidently saw it as a fund to be dipped into. The King, on the other hand viewed it as part of his accounts. At the end

Philip Mountbatten celebrates with Naval friends and his Uncle Louis, the night before his wedding.

of October, it was decided, after all, to set up a Select Committee.

THE KING'S BEST OFFER

On November 7, Dalton proposed that the Palace should hand over the £200,000 to the government which would then pay out £10,000 a year to the Princess, additional to the £15,000 that she was already receiving. Meanwhile, also out of this money would be paid £5,000 to Philip. The Palace was furious but Dalton returned for a meeting on November 10, claiming that he had expected the King to turn it down and that it was no more than a bargaining position.

Then at a Cabinet meeting the day after an austere budget, a message from the King was read out in which he said he was happy to "place at the disposal of the faithful Commons a sum derived from savings on the Civil List made during the war years." The proposal was unanimously accepted, even the left-wing socialists admitting that they did not want standards to slip regarding the monarchy. It was hoped that the Select Committee would come to some quick conclusions and the matter could be ended.

But things that night took a strange turn. Hugh Dalton was accused of being the source of a leak of some budget information that was published while he was on his feet in the Commons delivering his Budget speech. It had been inadvertent but he was forced to resign. No doubt, there were some wry smiles at the Palace.

Dalton's replacement Stafford Cripps (1889 – 1952) pushed through a generous provision for the Princess—£50,000 which included an increase of £25,000 for her and Philip was to receive £10,000. Furthermore, the King was asked to hand over only £100,000 of the wartime savings for four years. Parliamentary approval was still required, however, and the new provision only just made it through the vote.

A PEOPLE SO DEAR TO ME

Wedding presents flooded in from all over the world and the extravagant gifts were exhibited to the public at St. James's Palace for an entry fee of a shilling. The Emperor of Ethiopia Haile Selassie gave the Princess a golden tiara, Chinese leader Chiang Kai-shek sent a 176-piece porcelain dinner service, and the Aga Khan III sent her a chestnut filly.

Before the wedding, the Princess spent days visiting corporate donors and thanking them. Her speech at such events included the words:

> *As long as we live, it will be the constant purpose of Lieutenant Mountbatten and myself to serve a people who are so dear to me and to show ourselves deserving of their esteem.*

A wedding cake had to be chosen and it attracted almost as much interest as the wedding itself. Cake manufacturers with links to the royal family were asked to make a cake in return for an invitation to the party at which all the cakes could be examined and tasted. It was to be in the State dining room at the palace and the King and Queen would be present. Twelve cakes were presented for discussion and exposure to the royal taste buds. They were opulent, the largest one, which took four months to make, standing more than four feet tall.

Then there was the dress. Shortages made this into a challenge. Norman Hartnell (1901 – 79) made it of what he called "clinging ivory silk." It bore many small pearls with jasmine, smilax, seringa, and rose-like blossoms. The dress was displayed like the presents and created long lines of people waiting to see it.

THE REMNANTS OF EUROPEAN ROYALTY

What remained of European royalty after the war arrived in London, impoverished and stripped of their status. They regarded Prince Philip as a sign of hope for the future.

Norman Hartnell

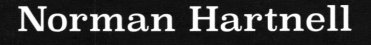

Fashion designer Norman Bishop Hartnell (1901 – 79) was best known as the designer of choice for the ladies of the royal family. He gained the Royal Warrant as Dressmaker to Queen Elizabeth, the Queen Mother in 1940 and to Queen Elizabeth II in 1957. In the years between the wars, he was responsible for making London a center of fashion. Born in Streatham in London, he read Modern Languages at Cambridge University before working unsuccessfully for two London designers. He launched his own dressmaking company in Mayfair in 1923.

Soon, he had developed a prosperous business, making dresses for numerous celebrities and film stars. But in 1926 when he showed his collection in Paris, it was a disaster. He was told his dresses were beautiful but very badly made. So he went back to London to learn the art of making clothes. He did not return to Paris until 1929. He was commissioned to design the dresses for the wedding of the Duke of Gloucester, George V's youngest son, which meant he would be dressing Princess Elizabeth and Princess Margaret.

The Queen Mother loved his clothes and he designed her entire wardrobe for the 1938 visit she made with her husband to Paris. He designed Princess Elizabeth's wedding dress and later the outfit she wore for her Coronation. He wrote of the Coronation garments: "I thought of the sky, the earth, the sun, the moon, the stars and everything heavenly that might be embroidered on a dress destined to be historic." Emblems of the home nations were also incorporated.

Throughout the 1950s, he continued to design for the Queen's royal tours. In the 1960s he attempted to update the Queen's and the Queen Mother's style with shorter hemlines, but the fashion revolution of Biba and Mary Quant made Hartnell and the other British designers of the time look out of date. Business began to suffer and he had to cut back on staff. "There just aren't the rich people these days," he said. The gossipy, amusing Norman Hartnell died in straitened circumstances in 1979, at the age of 77.

On her wedding day in 1947, Princess Elizabeth wore her flowing Norman Hartnell gown with Queen Mary's Fringe tiara. But just before she left for Westminster Abbey, the tiara snapped, and the court jeweler had to rush in for emergency repairs.

People who had not seen each other for decades, cousins and distant relatives met up again. Queen Alexandra of Yugoslavia recalled everyone "shedding their grown-up façade and romping together in an abandon of gossip, leg-pulling, and long-remembered family jokes." In fact, the royal family paid the traveling expenses of many of the less well-off royals who were invited.

Some were left off the guest list however, Philip's sisters, for example, who had married Germans. Most tricky of all was the decision not to invite the Duke of Windsor who spent his favorite niece's wedding day in a suite at the Waldorf Towers in New York. Those who were present enjoyed a grand dinner on the eve of the wedding. The financial difficulties many of those present were facing was evident in their dress and adornment, and Lady Airlie noted that "anyone fortunate enough to have a new dress drew all eyes."

THE GREAT DAY DAWNS

Several thorny issues had to be settled before the big day. What was Prince Philip going to be called and how should he be styled? It was decided that he should be Baron Greenwich—reflecting his naval background—Earl of Merioneth, and Duke of Edinburgh. It was also decided, after some research, to call him His Royal Highness. He was also granted a coat of arms which the King spent much time on. Philip then completed his journey to being a full Englishman at the end of September when he was received into the Church of England by the Archbishop of Canterbury at Lambeth Palace.

With such matters sorted, the great day dawned and found Princess Elizabeth very much as she was on the day of her father's Coronation. She stood in her dressing gown at a Buckingham Palace window, gazing out at the early morning traffic and the crowds that were already beginning to assemble in the Mall. Many had waited all night despite the cold

weather to catch a glimpse of the Princess as she rode to the Abbey in the state coach.

The wedding was broadcast to forty-two countries, as was noted by the Archbishop of York, officiating with the Archbishop of Canterbury, who said that although the wedding was followed by more people than any other in history, the actual ceremony was "in all essentials exactly the same as it would have been for a cottager who might be married this afternoon in some small country church in a remote village in the Dales."

There had been much debate about what the Princess would say when making her wedding vows and against the wishes of advocates of social equality, she did indeed promise "to love, cherish and obey" her husband. Two thousand people crowded into Westminster Abbey and Philip's cousin, the 3rd Marquess of Milford Haven, was Philip's best man.

LOVE-IN-THE-MIST BLUE

The couple signed the register in the Chapel of St. Edward the Confessor and after bowing and curtsying to the King and Queen, they climbed into the magnificent Glass Coach for the journey back to Buckingham Palace, where an "austerity" wedding breakfast was enjoyed by 150 of the guests at the end of which the King toasted the bride. The couple then left for Waterloo Station, the bride dressed in a coat of "love-in-the-mist blue," the Prince in naval uniform, cheered all the way by massive crowds of well-wishers.

The event was lovingly described on the radio by the BBC and the broadcast was listened to in many far-flung corners of the world. A select few were also able to watch it on the new medium of television. One camera captured the Princess's coach departing from the Abbey, another picked it up outside the Abbey. Inside, the service was captured, shown on television that same evening and flown to the United States for broadcast the following day.

Princess Elizabeth's wedding procession on the way to the church through central London on November 20, 1947.

The royal family group at the wedding of Princess Elizabeth and Prince Philip. In the family group are Lord Mountbatten, King George VI, Queen Elizabeth the Queen Mother, Queen Mary, and Princess Margaret.

CHAPTER 9

THE FUTURE OF THE MONARCHY

A honeymoon is normally a time for a young, newly-wed couple to get away on their own and become used to the new life they have undertaken. Not for this couple, however. The public were at a fever pitch of fascination and emotion and this could not just be stopped as soon as they left London. The idea was that the Duke and Duchess of Edinburgh, as they were called, would spend the beginning of their honeymoon at Broadlands, Uncle Dickie Mountbatten's Hampshire estate.

A huge crowd awaited them as they went to Sunday church at Romsey Abbey near the estate a few days after the wedding. Incredibly, after the royal party had left, people lined up to sit on the seats on which the royal posteriors had rested. After a week at Broadlands, some respite from the public gaze was found when they headed north to Birkhall in Scotland.

SUDDENLY A WOMAN

They returned to Buckingham Palace in time for the King's birthday. He was 52 on December 14. Jock Colville's impressions of the newly-wed Princess offer an insight:

> *The Edinburghs are back from Scotland. She was looking very happy, and, as a result of three weeks of matrimony, suddenly a woman instead of a girl.*

They had selected Sunninghill Park near Ascot as their country home, but it was gutted by fire before they could move in. Instead they leased Windlesham Moor, a house near Sunningdale in Surrey that would only be available at weekends. During the week they would stay in London, in Stable Yard at Clarence House, near Buckingham Palace.

However, Clarence House had been allowed to deteriorate by the elderly Duke of Connaught and had been damaged by bombs in the London Blitz during the Second World War. So they had to live at Buckingham Palace while it was being refurbished. They finally moved in the following summer. It suited Prince Philip whose new job as Director of Operations at the Admiralty was just a short walk away.

THE PROMISE OF BETTER DAYS

The Princess and the Duke had separate bedrooms at Clarence House but they were connecting and while they were getting dressed for an evening function, Bobo MacDonald helping her, his valet, John Dean helping him, they could chat with each other between rooms.

Early in 1948, it was announced that Elizabeth was expecting her first child which, if a boy, would become second in the line of succession to the throne. It did not become public knowledge, however, until the summer. Nonetheless, she was busy, the furor of the wedding having seemingly increased the hunger for her presence at events and functions.

There was no doubt that the eyes of the nation were watching her every move. She was seen not only as the future of the monarchy but as an emblem of the country. Things were more hopeful in Britain by then, and Elizabeth was a symbol of that improvement in fortune. Her wedding was the promise of better days ahead.

At the same time, life was an endless round of being seen in pretty clothes, cutting ribbons and giving innocuous speeches. A pretty aimless existence. Jock Colville began to try to make her more politically aware, including her in the distribution of Foreign Office telegrams. He also took her on educational excursions.

They watched a debate on foreign affairs at the House of Commons. Initially, he found her lacking in interest but he persevered, taking her to a juvenile court. She dined with a group of Labour MPs and their wives, spending time in conversation with each of them. She did, however find the evening very difficult.

BONDING WITH THE FRENCH

Jock Colville proposed a visit to Paris by the Princess and the Duke in an attempt to strengthen bonds with the French. The King and the government agreed it would be a good plan. Elizabeth was excited by the idea, but Philip who had spent a part of his childhood in France, was less than thrilled by the notion. He felt he was being railroaded into it. Colville had spoken to everyone else about it before asking him, but he eventually came round to the idea.

The centerpiece of the visit was the opening of the Exhibition of Eight Centuries of British Life at the Musée Gallera but the main point

Philip and Elizabeth on their honeymoon at Broadlands, the Mountbatten estate in Hampshire, November 1947.

was to bring Britain and France together after all the war years of turmoil. It was a huge success, Parisians turning out in droves to catch a glimpse of the Princess and her husband.

They enjoyed lunch at the Grand Trianon at Versailles before sailing down the Seine and dining at the British Embassy. Everywhere they went they were greeted by cheering crowds who were delighted with the Princess's flawless French, taught to her by the Vicomtesse de Bellaigue.

On returning home, the Princess was in even greater demand for engagements. Her French trip had cemented the view of her as a hope for a better future. This became even more the case when, on June 4, the day of the Derby horserace, it was announced that she was expecting her first child.

Elizabeth surprised many and broke royal protocol by appearing at Epsom racecourse for the Derby that afternoon regardless of her condition. Following the announcement, gifts and baby clothes started to pour in for the baby from all over the world.

THE KING IN DECLINE

It was around this time that the health of George VI started to become an issue. He had been unwell for some time, but became worse in the fall of 1948. Doctors examined him on October 30, and he was found to be suffering from arteriosclerosis—the narrowing of the arteries.

There was also the threat of gangrene and the doctors were contemplating the amputation of his right leg. The full consequences were kept from His Majesty and Princess Elizabeth herself only knew that her father was unwell, in pain, and that her mother was very worried.

But, despite the situation, there was an important constitutional issue to be settled. On November 9, Sir Alan Lascelles informed His Majesty that if the Princess gave birth to a son, he would be titled Earl of Merioneth; if she gave birth to a daughter, her title would be Lady [her given name] Mountbatten.

If they were to be styled "HRH Prince" or "HRH Princess" Letters Patent would have to be prepared before the child's birth. That same day, Letters Patent were issued to the effect that the child would be "HRH" and enjoy the title of "Prince."

THE END OF AN ARCHAIC CUSTOM

For centuries it had been the custom for the Home Secretary to be present at the birth of an heir to the throne. The practice was introduced to prevent any substitution or confusion regarding the child's identity.

In 1926, when Princess Elizabeth was born, the Home Secretary was William Joynson-Hicks, popularly known as "Jix." Initially his attendance at the birth had been considered and the King had said that the custom should be maintained, but he changed his mind in November. The King and Queen were said to have made the decision to end the practice in a demonstration of their modernity.

But it was not the aspiration to be seen as modern that had changed the King's view on the subject. The truth was that the Canadian High Commissioner, L. Dana Wilgress (1892 – 1969) had pointed out to him that as the new baby would be their king or queen too, then representatives of all the Dominions should be present as well as the British Home Secretary. This was constitutionally correct, although no one had realized it before.

The King was horrified at the prospect of seven officials of various governments from around the world attending the birth, so on November 5, 1926, it was quietly announced that the custom was being discontinued.

A ROYAL ARRIVAL

Clarence House was still not ready. Therefore, it was decided that the Princess should give birth at Buckingham Palace. The room chosen was just below the second-floor bedroom and had windows that looked out onto the Mall. She went into labor on November 14, and four doctors supervised the birth of a boy just after nine o'clock.

The Duke of Edinburgh was on the squash court at the time of his son's birth. When he was told, he immediately went to his wife and then saw his son for the first time in the Palace nursery.

The crowd that gathered in the Mall was so large that the road had to be cordoned off. They remained there cheering until after midnight. The newspapers provided full details of the child and lead articles emphasized the virtue of having a monarchy.

The photographer Cecil Beaton (1904 – 80) was summoned to the Palace a few days later to take the first official photographs of royal mother and royal baby. He reported:

> Prince Charles, as he is to be named, is an obedient sitter. He interrupted a long, contented sleep to do my bidding and open his blue eyes to stare long and wonderingly into the camera lens, the beginning of a lifetime in the glare of publicity.

Meanwhile on the instructions of the Princess, the food parcels that had arrived at the Palace were distributed to mothers of children born on the same day as Charles.

LETTERS PATENT

Letters Patent are a vestige of extra-parliamentary power by a monarch or president, a remnant of when a ruler ruled absolutely. They are nowadays a legal instrument for a written order by a monarch, a president, or head of state that grant a title, an office, a right, a monopoly or status to an individual or to a corporation.

No government approval is required; merely the signature of the monarch. They might be employed to create government offices, or the granting of city status, or a coat of arms. Representatives of the Crown are nominated through Letters Patent. For the United Kingdom these could be the appointment of governors-general of Commonwealth countries. They can also be used to appoint a Royal Commission. Peers of the realm are created using Letters Patent.

Princess Elizabeth with Prince Charles, photographed by Cecil Baton, 1948.

Cecil Beaton

Not only was Cecil Walter Hardy Beaton (1904 – 1980) a fashion, portrait, and war photographer, he was also a painter, interior designer, and Oscar-winning stage and costume designer for films and theater. Born the son of a timber merchant in Hampstead, London, he learned the rudiments of photography from his nanny at an early age. He went to Harrow School and St. John's College, Cambridge, where he studied history, art, and architecture but persevered with photography, having a portrait published in *Vogue*.

His first exhibition caused a sensation and his career took off. He worked for *Vogue* from 1927 and photographed the "Bright Young Things" of the 1920s and 1930s. Beaton was never the most technical of photographers, but had the skill of being able to compose a model or a scene to capture the right moment. He is best known for his fashion photographs and portraits of notable society figures. His photos appeared in both *Vanity Fair* and *Vogue* but he was fired by the latter after inserting tiny anti-Semitic phrases into a picture in American *Vogue*. The issue had to be reprinted.

Returning to England, the Queen recommended him as a war photographer to the Ministry of Information and he took many iconic photographs of the Blitz. The royal family often employed him and the Queen Mother was his favorite subject. He was also the official photographer at the wedding of the Duke of Windsor and Wallis Simpson in June 1937 in France.

After the war ended, Beaton began designing for theater and film. He designed the costumes for the 1964 film *My Fair Lady* as well as a number of others. He died in 1980 at the age of 76.

THE KING'S ILLNESS

The King's health continued to worry the royal family. A proposed visit to New Zealand and Australia was cancelled. It was a significant time for Princess Elizabeth as the full implications of her father's illness began to sink in.

The King had prematurely aged although still only in his early 50s, which contrasted greatly, of course, with the Princess who with her new baby was a source of optimism for the public. He remained a devoted family man but his ability to deal with matters of state—never great at the best of times—became diminished as he became increasingly frail.

He also became frustrated and obstinate in such matters and his staff found him difficult. It was always politics that brought out the worst in him, his "Hanoverian bark" as one guest at Sandringham and Balmoral recalled. Some suggested that his outbursts were merely attempts to cover up his inadequacies. An advisor shared an insight:

He had his explosions. He would explode if he read something in the paper that the Prime Minister hadn't told him about. We used to call them his 'gnashes.' When they occurred Princess Margaret was very good at defusing them.

HIGH SOCIETY

The King underwent major surgery on his spine at Buckingham Palace in March 1949, doctors trying to restore the circulation to his leg. By June, although a semi-invalid, he was well enough to watch the Trooping the Color ceremony, with Princess Elizabeth taking the salute in his place.

The time remaining to him was filled with illnesses and short periods of good health. The Queen found it hard to face up to what was actually going on, as one aide said: "The Queen never allowed you to contemplate the fact of the King's illness."

Princess Elizabeth, the Duke of Edinburgh, and Princess Margaret attending a Charity Ball at the Dorchester Hotel, London, 1948.

Princess Elizabeth had no option but to rise to the occasion as her father's health visibly deteriorated and he began to look like a tired old man. Her responsibilities increased but she and the Duke of Edinburgh also engaged in an active and exciting social life.

They attended parties with other members of high society and were often seen in the company of the celebrities of the day. On the day of Princess Elizabeth's twenty-third birthday, for instance, she dined at the fashionable Café de Paris restaurant with Laurence Olivier (1907 – 89) and Vivien Leigh (1913 – 67) who had starred in the play *The School for Scandal* that she had seen earlier that night at the New Theater in London's West End.

A NAVAL OFFICER'S WIFE

Clarence House was at last ready and in the summer of 1949 the Princess and the Duke moved in. Finally they were in their own home as a family but everything was soon turned upside-down. The Duke of Edinburgh had been working at the Royal Naval Staff College at Greenwich, but in October of that year, he was given a new assignment. He was to be First Lieutenant and second-in-command of the ship HMS *Chequers,* a C-Class destroyer and leader of the 1st Destroyer Squadron based at Malta.

He flew to Malta on October 16 with the Princess due to join him there after a few weeks. It was an extraordinary time for a young woman brought up in the cloistered existence of royal life. Crawfie suggested that she "saw and experienced for the first time the life of an ordinary girl." Lieutenant-Commander Mike Parker (1920 – 2001), who in 1947 had been appointed Equerry to the royal couple, described it as:

> *... a fabulous period when it was thought a good idea for her to become a naval officer's wife. It seemed the King's wish that she should do so.*

A ROUSING SPEECH

In the meantime, the Princess was busy being a working mother. She addressed a Mothers' Union gathering at Central Hall, Westminster, a speech that was to reinforce the Mothers' Union condemnation of divorce. The Princess complained in her speech about the "current age of growing self-indulgence, of hardening materialism, of falling standards." She talked of the suffering caused to children of broken marriages:

> *... we can have no doubt that divorce and separation are responsible for some of the darkest evils in our society today.*

She worried that children would follow the example of their parents and exhorted them to be unafraid of being judged "priggish" and to say and do what they believed to be the right thing.

Naturally, the speech roused the anger of those seeking to change the divorce laws who insisted that a royal voice had no place in such a discussion and that the Princess had appeared to be simply endorsing the conservative views of the Mothers' Union. It was suggested that her image and position had been exploited to get the message across but one Palace insider insisted that:

> *King George and Queen Elizabeth were completely satisfied that their daughter had been right, for their views on marriage and family were the same.*

MALTA AND MOUNTBATTEN

On November 20, Princess Elizabeth flew to Malta. While some said she might for once live the life of an ordinary woman, it is worth noting that traveling along with her was a small entourage of servants—a lady-in-waiting, Lady Alice Egerton (1923 – 77) daughter of the 4th Earl of Ellesmere, as well as Mike Parker, Bobo MacDonald, and John Dean, her husband's valet. Her one-year-old son was left in the care of her nursery staff in England.

In Malta, Elizabeth did lead a more normal life, having tea and dining with others who had been posted there. Philip was happy to have returned to the navy life he loved and to a job he knew he had on merit and not through having married his wife. She drove a Daimler on her own or sometimes with a friend around the island. She might go and watch the Duke of Edinburgh take part in a sporting event or go sailing and swimming.

In addition, Princess Elizabeth's life was made very much more comfortable by the presence of Lord Mountbatten who was commander of the 1st Cruiser Squadron of the Mediterranean Fleet, and may have had a hand in Philip's posting to Malta. He allowed the royal couple to use his house on Malta, Villa Guardamangia. Elizabeth remained there until her husband's ship was sent to patrol the Red Sea at the end of December. Not quite the overseas armed forces life that the other Navy wives were experiencing.

When Elizabeth returned home to England, she did not immediately rush to be with her young son, going firstly to Clarence House before heading to the races at Hurst Park in Surrey. There, she watched Monaveen win, a racehorse she co-owned with her mother. Finally, she traveled to Sandringham to be reunited with her son and her parents.

A SECOND ROYAL BABY

The Princess's twenty-fourth birthday was spent in Malta, watching her husband and Uncle Dickie play polo. That month it was also announced that she was having another baby, due in August. This time, she would give birth at Clarence House and once again crowds gathered outside for hours. On August 15, 1950, a little girl named Anne was born.

Elizabeth's recovery took a while and she was advised to rest until October before resuming her duties. A heavy cold in November delayed her return to work, however. Toward the end of that month, she flew to Malta. She spent Christmas there with her husband while her children spent Christmas with their grandparents at Sandringham.

Promoted to Lieutenant-Commander, the Duke of Edinburgh was given command of the frigate HMS *Magpie*. The *Magpie* provided an escort for the Commander-in-Chief's dispatch vessel, HMS *Surprise*, during a visit to King Paul and Queen Frederika of Greece. King Paul was a cousin of the Duke.

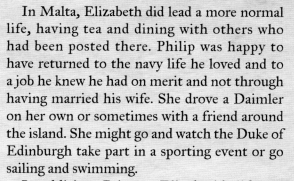

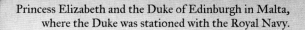

Princess Elizabeth and the Duke of Edinburgh in Malta, where the Duke was stationed with the Royal Navy.

CHAPTER 10

THE PASSING OF GEORGE VI

Princess Anne (left) and Prince Charles with their mother, Princess Elizabeth.

The King's increasing debilitation through illness meant more engagements for Princess Elizabeth. This began to make life in the navy difficult for Prince Philip. The management of a career in the navy with the need for him to be with his wife on official business was impossible. Therefore, he was forced to sacrifice his career. It was the first of many sacrifices the Prince made over the years.

Philip was just thirty and could easily have attained a high rank in the service but something had to give, as he knew only too well. He flew home from Malta in the summer of 1951 and never resumed his career. His valet said, "... he loved the sea and adored the Navy, and some of my gayest times with him were when he was serving."

He noted how the Prince could be "inclined to be moody and impatient" after he came home and it took him some time to come to terms with the situation. As ever, this was not helped by his dislike of the unbending royal establishment. A former courtier said:

Prince Philip was very hostile to Buckingham Palace, he didn't like it, and he wanted his own show.

INCREASING POLITICAL AWARENESS

Jock Colville left the couple to return to the Foreign Office and was replaced by Major Martin Charteris (1913 – 99). He would work for Elizabeth as Princess and Queen for the next twenty-seven years. It was a happy time at Clarence House. It seems the Princess was happy with her team and made them happy to be part of it. She and Philip often took lunch with the staff and things were less formal than could be expected at the Palace.

Charteris suggested that her political awareness might be increased if she were to see not only the Foreign Office telegrams arranged by Jock Colville but also Cabinet papers. He raised the matter with the Cabinet Secretary Sir Norman Brook (1902 – 67) and it was agreed with Prime Minister Clement Attlee and the King that it should be trialled. Attlee soon suggested that it should be made permanent.

Meanwhile, the King was increasingly ill and the Princess was carrying out more royal duties on her own. When the time came for Trooping the Color, the King was too ill to attend and she undertook the ceremony on her own, riding side-saddle and dressed in the scarlet uniform of Colonel of the Grenadier Guards.

◄─◄─►─►

THE KING'S DIAGNOSIS

Exploratory surgery in September 1951 confirmed that the King was, as many had suspected, suffering from cancer and his left lung was removed. Steps were hurriedly taken to confirm the Princess, the Queen, the Duke of Gloucester, and the Princess Royal as Counsellors of State so that the business of the Monarchy could continue uninterrupted. It meant also that the King would not have to be troubled with such matters during his recuperation.

The first matter to be dealt with was a general election to be held on October 15. Eleven days before this date, the Princess attended the Privy Council that preceded the dissolution of Parliament. The tour of Australia and New Zealand that the King and Queen had been due to start in January was cancelled.

Princess Elizabeth riding side-saddle in the red uniform of the Grenadier Guards representing the King at Trooping the Color ceremony in London on June 7, 1951.

TOURING NORTH AMERICA

One tour that did take place was that of the Princess and Prince Philip to Canada and it was extended to take in a visit to the United States. They flew to Newfoundland on October 7—their first transatlantic flight—still deeply worried about the King's health.

This concern caused the Princess some problems, the Canadian press claiming that she looked bored or distracted at times and did not smile. A special train was used as in South Africa, and the Canadian people became very excited about seeing the royal couple, traveling huge distances to catch a glimpse of them.

On October 23, they flew to Washington DC where President Truman had given all federal employees time off to go and see the couple. In fact, Truman seemed to adore the Princess and it was said that when he appeared beside her in public, he gave "the impression of a very proud uncle presenting his favorite niece to his friends."

The streets were lined with cheering crowds and the newspapers gushed about "little Lilibet" who had "suddenly matured into the lovely young mother who one day is to be the ruling Queen of England."

CHANGE IS IN THE AIR

Remarkably, the 1951 election returned a Conservative government which although it polled less votes in total, won enough seats to have a working majority. Even more remarkably, Winston Churchill would once again be the Prime Minister in 10 Downing Street. It was a result that pleased the King and Queen. Churchill was now 77, but the King found it reassuring to have him back. They had formed a tight bond during the war years.

At Sandringham that Christmas, the King was delighted to have prerecorded his Christmas broadcast, meaning he did not have the stress of delivering it live. But he looked a shadow of the man he had been, gaunt and pale. He managed to go shooting and was planning to travel with

the Queen to South Africa in March. He had been offered the use of Botha House, the South African Prime Minister's country residence to convalesce.

Elizabeth and the Duke of Edinburgh flew to Kenya on January 31, the first stage of their trip to Australia and New Zealand. Unusually, the King had escorted them to Heathrow airport to bid them farewell. It would be the last time he would see his daughter.

Churchill, who accompanied him to the airport, said that he was "gay and even jaunty; [he] drank a glass of champagne. I think he knew he had not long to live." He said to Bobo, "Look after the Princess for me, Bobo."

MASTER OF HER FATE

George VI passed away suddenly in his sleep six days later on February 6, 1952. Princess Elizabeth was watching animals from a platform in the branches of a giant fig tree at the Treetops Hotel in Aberdare National Park, Kenya.

Still unaware of events in London, she and her husband returned to Sagana Lodge to start preparing for their journey to Mombassa where they were to board the SS *Gothic* for the journey to New Zealand.

Martin Charteris was told that the King had died by a journalist at a hotel where he was having lunch. He telephoned the lodge to pass the news to Michael Parker. Parker crept around the outside of the building and caught the attention of Prince Philip. Philip was shocked, as Parker later recalled. "He looked as if you'd dropped half the world on him. I never felt so sorry for anyone in all my life."

The Princess was informed by Philip that she was Queen at 2:45 p.m., local time. She took it as well as could be expected, Martin Charteris describing her as "very composed, absolute master of her fate." Charteris asked her what she was going to call herself as Queen. "My own name, of course," she replied.

HIS MAJESTY
KING GEORGE VI

George VI (1895 – 1952) was King of the United Kingdom and the Dominions of the British Commonwealth from 1936 to 1952. He became King after his brother Edward VIII abdicated.

PART THREE

A NEW ELIZABETHAN AGE

For the first time in the history of the world, a young girl climbed into a tree one day a Princess and after having what she described as her most thrilling experience she climbed down from the tree next day a Queen — God bless her.

Jim Corbett, Royal Bodyguard,
Treetops Hotel, Kenya

CHAPTER 11

BECOMING THE WORLD'S QUEEN

After word of George VI's death reached the new Queen, she and Prince Philip returned immediately to Britain. The Princess always traveled with mourning clothes in case of just such an eventuality and they were waiting for her at Entebbe. On the airplane journey she and everyone else appeared calm. Charteris was going through what she could expect when she returned to Britain.

They landed at London's Heathrow airport in mid-afternoon and there to meet them were the Duke of Gloucester and the Mountbattens. They boarded the plane to greet the new Queen privately. An equerry brought a note from Queen Mary for Elizabeth. Winston Churchill awaited her somberly on the tarmac, overcome with emotion and unable to speak. A black Rolls Royce took her home to Clarence House.

The following morning, February 8, the Accession Council met at St. James's Palace.

Elizabeth "a slight figure dressed in deep mourning," as one attendee recalled, "entered the great room alone, and with strong but perfectly controlled emotion, went through the exacting task the Constitution prescribed." She read her Declaration of Sovereignty to the assembled Privy Council and then added: "My heart is too full for me to say more to you today than that I shall always work as my father did." The Duke of Edinburgh led her out to the waiting car and only then, apparently did she shed tears.

QUEEN ELIZABETH, THE QUEEN MOTHER

In the afternoon, Elizabeth and Philip drove to Sandringham where her father's body lay. As a friend recalled four decades later, the former Queen was grief-stricken:

The new Queen, Elizabeth II, returns from Kenya following the death of King George VI, February 7, 1952.

She was absolutely heartbroken; for a few months I thought she wasn't going to pull herself together. I'm sure she thinks about him a great deal now, still misses him.

Eventually, she released a statement to the nation, saying that she would be called "Queen Elizabeth, the Queen Mother" and asking for "loyalty and devotion" and "protection and love" for her daughter in the task that lay ahead. She went to Scotland to stay with friends and discovered a beautiful but dilapidated castle. She purchased it and renamed it the Castle of Mey. There she would find the peace and tranquility she sought to recover from the loss of her husband.

It must have been very strange for the Queen Mother to suddenly find herself thrust into the background while her daughter moved to center-stage and became the focus of attention. Some have suggested that she was even a bit envious of her daughter. One Palace source said:

... she lived completely in her own little world and also resented and was terribly jealous of her daughter becoming Queen so that at one blow not only did she lose the King but the whole of the happiest and gayest family life of anyone one knows all fell to pieces at the same time.

MANAGING THE ROYAL CHANGES

It was a precarious situation and the new Queen was always conscious of paying respect to her mother in public, entering functions together, for example and not usurping her

THE ACCESSION COUNCIL

On the death of a monarch, the ceremonial body, the Accession Council, assembles in St. James's Palace to formally proclaim the accession of the next monarch to the throne. Through the Act of Settlement of 1701, a new monarch succeeds automatically and the Accession Council provides a confirmation of the successor. The Council's members are Privy Counsellors, Great Officers of State—such as the Great Lord Chamberlain, the Lord Privy Seal and the Lord High Admiral—members of the House of Lords, the Lord Mayor of the City of London, High Commissioners of the Commonwealth Realms, and senior civil servants.

The Privy Counsellors sign the Proclamation of Accession and this is then read out from the Friary Court balcony at St. James's Palace and then at various places in London, Edinburgh, Windsor, and York. When Queen Elizabeth II became Queen, the Council met twice as she was in Kenya when her father passed away. The first meeting was for the proclamation and the second was so that she could swear the oath that a new monarch takes. On accession, the new monarch has to make the Accession Declaration. This is made at the first state opening of Parliament after the accession or at the coronation, whichever takes place first.

Sir Gerald Wollaston, an officer of arms at the College of Arms, reads the Royal Accession Proclamation aloud following the death of King George VI, at Temple Bar, London, February 8, 1952.

mother's position as hostess at Sandringham or Balmoral. A courtier described their first Easter together at Windsor:

> *It was the first time they had lived under the same roof since the King died, and there was an awkwardness about precedence, the Queen not wanting to go in front of her mother and the Queen Mother being used to going first. According to Lascelles, the Queen Mother couldn't bear it—she was so young to be widowed and it wasn't likely she'd marry again and she minded the change of position although the Queen did everything possible to ease the situation.*

Meanwhile, for Princess Margaret everything changed. She had always been the apple of her father's eye. She had worshipped her father and his death was devastating for her.

COOKIE AND SHIRLEY TEMPLE

The Duke of Windsor had learned of his brother's death from reporters in New York where he was at the time. Having traveled to Britain on the *Queen Mary*, leaving his wife behind, he had tea with the Queen, Prince Philip, and the Queen Mother. He had been advised by his wife to try to achieve some sort of reconciliation with the Queen Mother. "I am sure," she wrote to him, "you can win her over to a more friendly attitude."

Nonetheless, the Queen Mother still blamed him and Wallis for her husband's early death. Relations with the family and his treatment by the courtiers in the Palace were on the surface friendly and correct, but as he wrote back to his wife: "... gee the crust is hard & only granite below."

But the Duke had his own reasons to be in London. The Palace had stopped paying him

The coffin of King George VI lies on a gun carriage drawn by naval officers, and accompanied by men of the Household Cavalry as the funeral procession passes through the streets of central London, February 15, 1952.

the £10,000 a year that had been arranged by his late brother and he had recently purchased a house in Paris—the Moulin des Tuileries. He wrote, "It's hell to be even this much dependent upon these ice-veined bitches ..."

In their correspondence, the Windsors used code for the members of the royal family. The Queen Mother was "Cookie" and the Queen was now "the girl," having been "Shirley Temple." But, the Queen had little time for her uncle's problems. She was busy meeting Commonwealth heads and other heads of state who had flown in for the funeral, slipping easily into her new role. The Duke of Windsor wrote that "Clarence House was informal & friendly. Brave New World, full of self-confidence & seem to take the job in their stride."

THE KING'S FUNERAL

In fact, the image being presented was of a new "Elizabethan Age." Indeed, Winston Churchill had heralded the new age in a moving Address of Sympathy in the House of Commons a few days before the funeral:

She comes to the Throne at a time when tormented mankind stands uncertainly poised between world catastrophe and a golden age. That it should be a golden age of art and letters, we can only hope—science and machinery have their tales to tell—but it is certain that if a true and lasting peace can be achieved, and if the nations will only let each other alone, an immense and undreamed of prosperity with culture and leisure ever more widely spread can come, perhaps even easily and swiftly, to the masses of people in every land. Let us hope and pray that the accession to our ancient Throne of Queen Elizabeth the Second may be the signal for such a brightening salvation of the human scene.

The funeral was held at St. George's Chapel, Windsor, on February 15, 1952. On a cloudy, misty morning, the mile-long cortege began its slow progress from Westminster Hall to the toll of fifty-six chimes from Big Ben, one for each year of the King's life. There were fifty-six gun salutes from Hyde Park and the Tower of London. It traveled along the Mall, passing Marlborough House where the King's mother, Queen Mary, watched from a window. It proceeded to Paddington railway station.

The Household Cavalry and pipers of the Scots Guards marched somberly in front of the Earl Marshal and some of the late monarch's servants. The coffin, on which rested the imperial crown, the orb and the Imperial Scepter was mounted on a gun carriage. Behind the Queen's carriage, containing her, her mother and her sister, walked the Dukes of Edinburgh, Gloucester, Windsor, and Kent and they were followed by heads of state and other dignitaries.

A black day for the three Queens of England at George VI's funeral. From left to right: Princess Elizabeth (George VI's daughter) who had just become Queen Elizabeth II, Queen Mary (George VI's mother), and Queen Elizabeth (George VI's wife).

From Paddington, a train took the coffin to Windsor for burial at St. George's Chapel where the King's father and grandfather had been laid to rest. Many predecessors, such as Henry VIII and Charles I were also buried there. The wreath sent by the government was in the shape of the George Cross and had an inscription signed by Winston Churchill which was the same as the one on the Victoria Cross—"For Valor."

THE HOUSE OF WINDSOR

Prince Philip's life changed irrevocably when the Queen acceded to the throne. He had to move to Buckingham Palace for a start, something he did only reluctantly. He probably saw this as curbing, somewhat, his freedom. His naval career was over and he was reduced really to being a man who walked a pace behind his wife at events and functions.

He had been made a Privy Counsellor, but the Queen had no intention of actually involving him in the business of ruling. While she was privy to official state papers and would meet, as her father had done, with the Prime Minister once a week, Philip was reduced to overseeing their estates and carrying out official duties.

The Queen also faced a difficult hurdle with Prince Philip—the name of the dynasty she represented. The problem arose from a conversation that Queen Mary had with her husband's cousin Prince Ernst of Hanover (1887 – 1953). He had been to a party at Lord Mountbatten's Broadlands country estate, at which Mountbatten had boasted that "the House of Mountbatten now reigned." This was because Elizabeth had married a Mountbatten. She passed the information to Jock Colville who reassured her that it was doubtful if this would be permitted.

Colville told Winston Churchill and the Cabinet was summoned to a meeting. The Cabinet wholeheartedly agreed that the royal family should continue to use the name Windsor. Five days after the King's funeral, the Queen told Churchill that she and her descendants would continue to bear the name Windsor.

WHAT IS A CONSORT?

A consort is the husband or wife of a ruling monarch. The title is symbolic and, in fact, the Duke of Edinburgh has never been officially designated Prince Consort or King Consort which are the official names for the role. There have been historical precedents, however. Queen Victoria, for instance, wanted to make her husband Albert King Consort but because he was a foreigner, the British government refused to introduce a bill that would have allowed it. Instead, in 1857 she named him as Prince Consort. Normally, as in the case of George VI's wife, Elizabeth, the consort, if he or she survived the monarch, would be known as Queen Mother or Father or King Mother or Father.

Elizabeth Bowes-Lyon (1900 – 2002) was Queen Consort to King George VI from 1936 until his death in 1952, when her elder daughter, Elizabeth, age 25, became the new Queen, after which she became known as The Queen Mother. She was viewed as the matriarch of the British royal family and continued an active public life until her death at the age of 101.

Her Majesty Queen Elizabeth was Queen Consort to George VI.

Apparently, as the Lord Chancellor drafted a pronouncement on the matter, Prince Philip had a major argument with him at Sandringham. Philip also wrote a memo expressing his disquiet at using Windsor instead of Mountbatten.

Churchill was deeply irritated by this and a reply was written on March 12 that rejected his points. It was decided to simply draft a declaration by the Queen that would be published in the *London Gazette*, the periodical for all such announcements. Thus, on April 7 the notice appeared, saying:

> *I hereby declare My Will and Pleasure that I and My children shall be styled and known as the House and Family of Windsor, and that my descendants who marry and their descendants shall bear the name Windsor.*

A SERIOUS LOSS OF IDENTITY

There were suspicions that Lord Mountbatten fancied himself as the power broker behind the throne and certainly he was an ambitious man. It was also believed by some that the Mountbattens were vying for Philip to be declared King or King Consort. One source close to Philip, however, insisted that the Duke of Edinburgh was fully cognizant of his uncle's machinations. But Philip did agree with Mountbatten on the issue of the family name.

Many thought Elizabeth had been bullied by Winston Churchill on the matter, but her family also did not want a change of name and that would certainly have been an important factor in her decision. There were other elements, though, especially the points made by the Lord Chancellor:

> *It cannot be doubted that by his Proclamation of 1917 George V intended that, so long as there was a member of His House to ascend the Throne, the name of the House should be Windsor.*

"I'm nothing but a bloody amoeba," Prince Philip exclaimed, complaining about what he saw as a serious loss of identity. His wife was growing ever more confident and he saw his role diminishing. One relative sympathized with him:

> *I think psychologically it was a terrible blow, because [the] poor young man felt already that everyone was giving him a hard time and there he was being told that his own children couldn't take his name. It was really hurting and it took him a long time to get over that one.*

It must have placed a strain on the royal marriage too, and when the consort's throne was removed from the House of Lords, Philip must have thought that the protocol was being adhered to only to slight him. It was erroneously believed that the throne could be used only by a female consort and that he should sit instead on a chair at a lower level than the monarch.

THE CORONATION COMMISSION

Perhaps with the aim of pacifying her husband, the Queen insisted that he became chair of the Coronation Commission, the body planning her Coronation. A date had to be settled upon, but 1952 was a non-starter due to the dire economic situation the country faced. As Churchill quipped: "Can't have Coronations with the bailiffs in the house." Finally, June 2, 1953, was chosen despite some controversy as it was the day before the Epsom Derby.

Apart from the Duke of Edinburgh, the Commission consisted of the Duke of Norfolk as vice-chairman and representatives of all the Commonwealth governments. Norfolk, as Earl Marshal, had previous experience, having organized George VI's coronation and his funeral. Philip tried to adopt a modern approach to the event, but found it difficult to get anything past his more conservative vice-chairman.

The first decision was a poor one for instance, the refusal to allow television cameras inside Westminster Abbey during the actual ceremony. Owners of TV sets had to be satisfied

THE KOH-I-NOOR DIAMOND

One of the world's most infamous diamonds, the Koh-i-Noor has a bloody history of ownership. The large 105-carat jewel now sits resplendent in the middle of the front cross of the Queen Mother's Crown. Made by Garrard & Co., the Crown Jeweler at the time, it was designed for Queen Elizabeth the Queen Mother to wear at the coronation of George VI in 1937.

The Koh-i-Noor, a large, colorless diamond was discovered in Andhra Pradesh in India probably in the thirteenth century. Owned initially by the Kakatiya dynasty in south India, the diamond changed hands many times in the next few centuries during the ravages of subsequent rulers. By 1526 its owner was Babur (1483 – 1530), the Turco-Mongol founder of the Mughal Empire that extended over large parts of the Indian subcontinent and Afghanistan.

The fifth Mughal emperor, Shah Jahan (1592 – 1666), had it set in his fantastically ornate Peacock Throne but when the Persian Shah Nader Shah (1698 – 1747) invaded in 1739, the treasury was looted and the Koh-i-Noor fell into his possession. He is said to have shouted "Koh-i-Noor!" (Mountain of Light) when he got his hands on it, which is how it acquired its name.

No one knows quite how he got it, but by 1808 the diamond was being worn as part of a bracelet by Shah Shujah Durrani (1785 – 1842) the sadistically cruel, self-proclaimed Emir of Afghanistan. In 1813 following his overthrow and in return for sanctuary from his enemies, Shujah gave the diamond to the founder of the Sikh Empire, Maharaja Ranjit Singh (1780 – 1839), who ruled the north-west Indian subcontinent in the early half of the nineteenth century.

Finally, when the Kingdom of Punjab was annexed by the British, the Koh-i-Noor passed into the possession of Queen Victoria as a spoil of war. The stone was cut and polished in 1852. It was set in the Crown of Queen Alexandra, wife of Edward VII, and worn at the Coronation of 1902.

In 1911 it was set in Queen Mary's Crown and then, in the Queen Mother's Crown for George VI's coronation. It is likely to be seen next when Camilla, Duchess of Cornwall will, in all likelihood, wear it at Prince Charles's coronation as the future King Charles III.

The Queen Mother's Crown is made of platinum and decorated with about 2,800 diamonds, most notably the Koh-i-Noor in the middle of the front cross. The crown is on public display along with the other Crown Jewels in the Jewel House at the Tower of London.

THE GOLD STATE COACH

The Gold State Coach is a magnificently ornate enclosed carriage drawn by eight horses. It was commissioned in 1760, costing £7,562 (approximately £1.4 million in today's money) and has been used in every coronation since that of George IV, a lavish affair that would have cost around £20 million today. Being very difficult to maneuver and weighing a great deal, it is used only on grand state occasions such as coronations, royal weddings and jubilees. Queen Elizabeth II used it on the occasion of both her silver and golden jubilees as well as at her Coronation.

Weighing four tons, and twenty-four feet in length and twelve feet high, the coach is gilded and has door panels painted by Giovanni Cipriani (1727 – 85). There are three gilded cherubs on the roof, representing Scotland, Ireland and England. At each of its four corners stands a triton, the mythological Greek god, which is symbolic of Britain's imperial power. The interior is lined with velvet and satin and its eight Windsor Greys wear a harness of red Morocco leather. The coach is driven by four postilions and it has nine walking grooms, six footmen, and four Yeomen of the Guard.

Queen Victoria would often refuse to ride in the coach due to its "distressing oscillation" and King George VI described his ride to his coronation at Westminster Abbey as "one of the most uncomfortable rides I have ever had in my life."

Queen Elizabeth II after her Coronation in the Gold State Coach which has been used at the coronation of every British monarch since George IV.

with a showing of this film later in the day. It has been suggested that Elizabeth had argued against this approach, but it has been shown since that she sided with those who supported tradition at all costs. Churchill, for his part, wondered if live broadcast on television would be too much for the young Queen but a note from Sir Jock Colville saying that she did not want it televised reassured him.

There was a backlash, however, and the press became very annoyed about the banning of television cameras. The public were also outraged. Finally, Sir Alan Lascelles came up with a compromise. Television cameras would be allowed into the Abbey but they could only film the service and not the communion. They would not be allowed to film the most sacred parts of the ceremony, the anointing, the communion prayers and the Queen's Communion.

CHURCHILL BLOCKS THE DUKE

One person who was not at the Coronation was Queen Mary who never really got over the death of her son and died on March 23, 1953, at age 85. A large crowd gathered outside her home, Marlborough House, and many wept at her passing. So there was another funeral at St. George's Chapel and Edward VIII, of course, attended. He had, however, not been invited to his niece's Coronation.

The Queen did not want him to attend but it was Churchill who saved everyone's embarrassment by informing the Duke that it would be "quite inappropriate for a King who had abdicated to be present as an official guest at the Coronation of one of his successors."

When he was summoned by the imminence of his mother's death, however, the former King was not in a good mood. This arose from the cutting off of his £10,000 annual gift by the Queen. His mood was further darkened by gossip in America that his wife was conducting an affair with a wealthy socialite nineteen years her junior, Jimmy Donoghue (1915 – 66).

He never came to terms with Queen Mary's attitude toward his abdication, the "Great Betrayal" as she called it, and his family never came to terms with him and his actions. He was not invited to the dinner that was held at Windsor Castle after the funeral on March 31. Furious at his treatment while in England, he wrote to his wife: "What a smug, stinking lot my relations are and you've never seen such a bunch of old hags most of them have become."

Queen Mary stipulated in her will that should she die before the Coronation, mourning for her

Mary of Teck (1867 – 1953) was Queen of the United Kingdom and Empress of India as the wife of George V. She died before her granddaughter Queen Elizabeth II was crowned.

should not be allowed to interfere with it. Thus the nation prepared for a huge party. Street parties and village carnivals were organized and to the delight of all, Churchill relaxed food rationing slightly by allowing everyone an extra pound of sugar. Restrictions on eggs and candies were also relaxed.

QUEEN ELIZABETH'S CORONATION

As if to support the notion that Britain was entering a brave new age, news came through on the eve of the Coronation that New Zealander Edmund Hillary (1919 – 2008) and the Nepalese Sherpa Tenzing Norgay (1914 – 86) had reached the summit of Mount Everest. It was viewed in some quarters as an achievement of the British Empire. The London *Evening Standard*, asked the question:

> *Does not the lesson of Everest stand out clear? ... while collectively and acting in unity the men of the Empire can conquer anything, singly they can conquer nothing. Long live the Queen! Long also may there live the Imperial unity which can make her reign one of peace and wondrous glory.*

Of course, this was somewhat contradictory to the government's message which was Commonwealth, not Empire. Elizabeth, too, wanted to emphasize the Commonwealth, requesting of her wedding-dress designer, Norman Hartnell, that he incorporate symbols of the countries of the Commonwealth, such as the lotus flower of Ceylon and the wattle of Australia. These were added to the symbols of England, Scotland, Ireland, and Wales.

She practiced with sheets pinned to her shoulders in imitation of the Coronation robes. She also wore the St. Edward's Crown which weighs five pounds, and was used for the actual crowning. In the Buckingham Palace ballroom, the floor was marked out with tape so that she could familiarize herself with the various positions she had to be in on the day.

AN ELECTRIC ATMOSPHERE

It rained on June 2, and was unseasonably cold but the atmosphere in London and the remainder of the country was electric. Thirty-thousand people lined the Mall as news of the conquest of Everest passed among them. Meanwhile, various carriages and cars passed by, the Lord Mayor of London in a coach, cars containing the royal family and many other royal dignitaries including the rather large form of Queen Solate of Tonga (1900 – 65) who was six feet three inches tall. She rode through the rain in an open-top carriage, getting wet, waving to people, and endearing herself to spectators along the way.

Elizabeth left the Palace in the spectacular Gold State Coach, wearing a white dress and Queen Victoria's diadem on her head. She also wore an ermine and velvet cloak with a train. Sitting beside her was the Duke of Edinburgh, dressed in the uniform of Admiral of the Fleet. On January 15, 1953, he had been promoted to this rank as well as Field Marshal and Air Chief Marshal. Just twelve years previously, he had joined HMS *Ramillies* as a plain midshipman. It had been a meteoric rise through the ranks.

The Gold State Coach arrived at Westminster Abbey at 11:00 a.m. precisely and Elizabeth climbed carefully down the carriage steps and made her way to a "retiring room." Meanwhile inside the Abbey since 9:00 a.m. that morning, there had been a series of processions up the aisle of foreign dignitaries and members of Europe's royal families.

Elizabeth entered the Abbey at 11:15 a.m. and there were already 7,500 guests in the pews. As choristers of Westminster shouted *"Vivat Regina!"* she walked up the aisle behind a procession of church figures, political leaders, and officials. Meanwhile, 4-year-old Prince Charles, in ordinary clothes, had entered the building through a side door, accompanied by his nanny.

THE CORONATION OF QUEEN ELIZABETH II

The Coronation of Queen Elizabeth II as monarch of the United Kingdom, Canada, Australia, New Zealand, South Africa, Pakistan, and Ceylon took place on June 2, 1953, at Westminster Abbey, London. Elizabeth ascended the throne at the age of 25, upon the death of her father, King George VI, on February 6, 1952, and was proclaimed Queen by her various privy and executive councils shortly afterward.

The Coronation took place more than a year later because of the tradition that holding such a festival is inappropriate during the period of mourning that follows the death of a monarch. During the service, she took and subscribed an oath to govern the people according to their respective laws and customs, was anointed with holy oil, presented and invested with regalia, and crowned.

THE CORONATION CEREMONY

The ceremony began. It is a ritual that has seen little change in more than a thousand years. The Coronation chair, known as St. Edward's Chair stood forebodingly as the centerpiece, housing the Stone of Scone which Edward I (1239 – 1307) had captured from Scotland in 1296. The stone is a rectangular lump of red sandstone, used for centuries at the coronation of Scottish kings and used since its capture for the coronation of English and then British monarchs.

The proceedings commenced with the Archbishop of Canterbury's proclamation to the bishops: "Sirs, I here present unto you Queen Elizabeth, your undoubted Queen." This was answered with shouts of "God save the Queen" and the sound of trumpets. The Archbishop asked her to swear:

To govern the peoples of the United Kingdom of Great Britain and Northern Ireland, Canada, Australia, New Zealand, the Union of South Africa, Pakistan and Ceylon and of your Possessions and the other Territories to any of them belonging or pertaining, according to their respective laws and customs.

Further oaths were sworn by her to judge with Law, Justice and Mercy, to maintain the laws of God and to protect the Church of England. To the singing of Handel's *Zadoc the Priest*, composed for the coronation of George II, the most sacred ritual of the ceremony took place.

With her crimson robe removed, leaving her in a simple white shift, the Archbishop anointed her with holy oil, declaring her to be "anointed, blessed, and consecrated Queen over the peoples, whom the Lord thy God hath given thee to rule and govern ..."

At this point of the ceremony, the peers of the realm approached Her Majesty to pay homage to her. Prince Philip was first, as one lady of the bedchamber recalled:

... and he must have made some amusing little joke, because it was the only time she smiled in the whole ceremony.

There were several small mistakes in the ceremony, just as there had been at her father's coronation. She forgot to curtsy at one moment and the Most Reverend Geoffrey Fisher (1887 – 1972), the Archbishop of Canterbury, moved forward at the wrong time. The wrong dish was offered by Very Reverend Alan Don, the Dean of Westminster, for the Queen's offering which consisted of a small bag of gold.

At last, however, it was over. The royal party traveled back to Buckingham Palace where photographs were taken by Cecil Beaton. Film of the Coronation was viewed by hundreds of millions around the world in the coming days and that night the new Queen broadcast to the nation.

THE WORLD'S QUEEN

The Queen wanted to be seen by her new subjects. She said, "I want to show that the Crown is not merely an abstract symbol of our unity but a personal bond between you and me." Therefore, just five or so months after her Coronation, she, her husband, and her close team, embarked on a mammoth five-and-a-half-month tour of the Commonwealth.

They visited Bermuda, Jamaica, Fiji, Tonga, New Zealand, Australia, the Cocos Islands, Ceylon, Uganda, Malta, and Gibraltar. It was a reworking of the trip that Elizabeth and Philip had begun the previous year that had ended so tragically at Treetops in Kenya.

After Bermuda and Jamaica, they traveled on the SS *Gothic* through the Panama Canal to Fiji and Tonga, a cruise lasting three weeks. They moved on to New Zealand, docking in Auckland to a welcome from huge crowds. While there, Elizabeth made her second Christmas broadcast live. Tours of North and South Islands ensued and thousands arrived to bid the royal party farewell on January 30, 1954.

The welcome was just as great in Sydney, Australia, where the harbor was filled with sailing craft. Their itinerary in Australia was exhausting as they traveled from one side of the vast country to the other, being seen, it is estimated by around 75 percent of the entire population.

They left Australia in April and headed for home, first interrupting the trip with a stop in Ceylon where on a humid day the Queen wore her glittering Coronation gown to open Parliament. When the glass beads in her dress became hot, she said it was "like being in a radiator."

They moved on to the British Protectorate of Aden and then to the East African colony of Uganda. Libya was next where they were reunited with Prince Charles and Princess Anne when they boarded the royal yacht *Britannia*. The Queen is reported to have quipped: "They were extremely polite. I don't think they knew who we were at all!" They sailed to Malta and then home to a rapturous welcome in Britain via Gibraltar.

The Queen makes her regal entry to the Hobart City Hall, Tasmania, for the Civic Ball, March 1954.

CHAPTER 12

PRINCESS MARGARET'S IMPOSSIBLE DREAM

Princess Margaret wearing her bridesmaid dress for her sister Elizabeth's marriage.

Queen Elizabeth II was fully aware, even before her Coronation, that her sister Princess Margaret was in love with a divorced man who was sixteen years older than her. The affair had the potential to cause as great a scandal as Edward VIII's love for Wallis Simpson had in 1936. Group Captain Peter Townsend was a war hero and had been a fighter pilot in the Second World War. He had been Equerry to George VI and performed the same role for Elizabeth. Unfortunately, the world also knew about the romance after Princess Margaret was spotted at the Coronation intimately brushing a piece of fluff off Townsend's RAF uniform.

The Queen initially had ignored the relationship, and when Sir Alan Lascelles tried to alert the Queen Mother, she became angry, leading him to do nothing more about it until it became too tricky to ignore. The late King, although he had seen evidence of the developing relationship, was hopeful that the Princess would get over it and marry one of the highly eligible young men who were part of Margaret's set.

They had hoped perhaps the Marquess of Blandford (1926 – 2014) whose seat was the splendid Blenheim Palace near Oxford would marry Margaret, but he married the W.H. Smith heiress, Susan Hornby in 1951. Or there was Johnny Dalkeith (1923 – 2007) who was heir to the Dukedom of Buccleuch with its vast estates and splendid houses. But Dalkeith chose to marry a former Norman Hartnell fashion model, Jane McNeill (1929 – 2011). Colin Tennant who was the son and heir of Lord Glenconner said later:

If the King had lived, he would have made Princess Margaret marry Johnny Dalkeith. With his houses and his land, she would have had a virtual state of her own.

AN IMPENDING FUROR

The rumors of a romance began as usual in the foreign press after Margaret had undertaken her first solo overseas trip, representing her sister at the Inauguration of Crown Princess Juliana as Queen of the Netherlands (1909 – 2004) on September 6, 1948. At the ball that followed the ceremony, it was noted how she danced with Group Captain Townsend and the closeness of the two was also noted as they toured the Rijksmuseum in Amsterdam the day after.

In his memoirs, Peter Townsend says that their relationship began after he was appointed Deputy Master of the Household and given his own office in 1951. By time, his marriage was a sham and he spent a lot of time in the Princess's company.

The truth was that they were both leading emotionally empty lives. Townsend's home life was miserable and Margaret's life was dull. She was a good-looking young woman and he was a handsome war hero, but many also thought her spoiled and arrogant. She was complicated, by turns kind and generous and then selfish and cruel. One courtier's wife said of her:

She had everything and then she destroyed herself. Her nature was to make everything go wrong. Nice one day—nasty the next. She was the only one who would come up to you at a party and really talk to you—then the next day she'd cut you. She antagonized her friends with her tricks, being horrid to their wives. She's come up to a man and get him to dance with her cutting out his wife ... Then she'd be so tiresome in house parties—keeping people up too late and buggering up evenings.

Princess Margaret and Group Captain Peter Townsend, equerry to King George VI, leaving Windsor Castle, April 1952.

Townsend, on the other hand, saw in her "a rare softness and sincerity." She gave him joy, he claimed. After her father's death, he became even more important to her. "Peter was always there for her," a friend said later. But most courtiers were horrified by the relationship and efforts were made to have him removed from his position.

He turned down a move to the Air Ministry. Indeed, after the Coronation he asked the Queen for another job because of the breakdown of his marriage. No mention was made to her of Margaret. She appointed him Comptroller of the Queen's Household.

In late 1952, he was granted a *decree nisi* against his wife Rosemary (1921 – 2004) who was having an affair. Townsend was now free and the couple were blissfully happy but naively unaware of the impending furor.

MAD OR BAD OR BOTH

When Princess Margaret broke the news of her love for Peter Townsend to her sister and her mother, the Queen Mother did as she had always done—she buried her head in the sand. She was regarded by courtiers as the "Royal Ostrich" because of her habit of not wishing to deal with anything nasty. The Queen, for her part, tried to be as sisterly as she could toward Margaret but she was well aware, as the head of a Church that did not recognize divorce, that trouble lay ahead.

The Royal Marriages Act of 1772 stipulated that, as sovereign, she would have to give her permission for them to marry, until Margaret reached the age of 25. Even then, she could marry within a year without Elizabeth's permission, but would still have to provide written notification to Parliament and both the House of Commons and the House of Lords would have to agree to the marriage. The Queen thought it not unreasonable to ask her sister to wait.

Sir Alan Lascelles who had experienced the trauma of the Abdication at close quarters, was horrified by the idea and was not slow in letting Group Captain Townsend know. "You must be either mad or bad or both," he is reported to have said on being told by Townsend.

The terminally naïve Townsend was very hurt by the reaction of a man he believed to be his friend. But when Townsend offered his resignation, Lascelles refused it, seeing that it would only give rise to even greater speculation. He recommended to the Queen that Townsend be transferred abroad but, instead, she had him moved from Clarence House to Buckingham Palace.

The day before the story of the affair was due to break in the British press, Lascelles drove to Chartwell, Churchill's country house, to inform him of the Princess's desire to marry Townsend. Churchill ordered a report on where the constitution stood on the matter of the Princess marrying a divorcee, and to informally gauge the response of Commonwealth Prime Ministers to the idea of the marriage. The Cabinet came to the conclusion that the Government could not condone it.

THE CAT IS OUT OF THE BAG

On June 14, *The People* newspaper boasted the headline "*The People* Speaks Out." It informed its readers of the affair, naming Townsend as the divorced man. Even though the piece conceded that he had been the innocent party in his divorce, it went on to insist loftily that "a marriage between Princess Margaret and himself would fly in the face of Royal and Christian tradition."

Townsend had to go, as the Queen was told by both her Press Secretary, Commander Richard Colville and Winston Churchill. Churchill added that it was probable that Cabinet would still not give its permission after the Princess reached 25. The Princess was not informed about any of this, something about which she was later very bitter.

Princess Margaret and Townsend agreed to the stipulation that they should separate and

Peter Townsend

Peter Wooldridge Townsend (1914 – 95) was born in Rangoon, Burma, the son of a lieutenant colonel in the British Army. In 1933, he joined the Royal Air Force and was commissioned as a pilot officer in 1935, joining No. 1 Squadron at RAF Tangmere in West Sussex. In 1936, he received a posting to No. 36 Squadron RAF in Singapore where he flew the Vickers Vildebeest torpedo bomber. Promoted to flying officer in 1937, he returned to Tangmere, joining No. 43 Squadron. Two years later, he was promoted again, this time to flight lieutenant.

Townsend was one of three pilots of fighters from RAF Acklington who downed the first enemy aircraft to crash on English soil in February 1940, when they brought down a Luftwaffe Heinkel 111. In the next few months he claimed two more Heinkels and in April 1940, was awarded the Distinguished Flying Cross (DFC).

In 1940, as commanding officer of No. 85 Squadron RAF, Townsend served with distinction through the Battle of Britain, flying Hawker Hurricanes. At one point, he was forced to ditch in the English Channel and was recused by HM Trawler *Cape Finisterre*. He was mentioned in dispatches. In August, he was shot down and wounded in the leg. His big toe was amputated, but he continued to lead his squadron, attaining the rank of squadron leader in September 1940.

The following month he had a bar added to his DFC for work protecting convoys during which he personally shot down four enemy aircraft. In 1941, he married Rosemary Pawle and they had two sons. By now he was an acting wing commander and was credited with the downing of eleven enemy aircraft. He was awarded the Distinguished Service Order (DSO). In April 1942, he became commanding officer of RAF Drew and commanded a Spitfire unit.

In 1944, Townsend was appointed Equerry to George VI and in 1953, he was made Extra Equerry, an honorary title that he held until his death. In 1950, he was made Deputy Master of the Household and in 1952 became comptroller to the Queen Mother. From 1953 until his retirement from the RAF in 1956, he was air attaché in Brussels.

In 1959, several years after his relationship with Princess Margaret ended, Townsend married a 20-year-old Belgian woman, Marie-Luce Jamagne. In later life he wrote a number of non-fiction books on various subjects, including the war and George VI. He died of stomach cancer in France in 1995 at age 80.

he would be sent to Brussels as air attaché. Meanwhile, on June 30, 1953, Margaret and the Queen Mother departed on a visit to Southern Rhodesia. Townsend and Margaret believed that he would not be sent away until she returned, but instead he was dispatched to his new post, on Churchill's orders, two days before she arrived back in Britain. When Margaret found out, she was devastated, and the Queen Mother had to carry out the remainder of their duties on her own.

WAIT AND SEE

In February and March of 1955, Princess Margaret undertook a very successful tour of the West Indies, during which she seemed reinvigorated. A day after her return home, however, an interview with Peter Townsend appeared in the *Daily Sketch*. He was asked bluntly whether he would be marrying the Princess and his reply "Wait and see" caused uproar. Townsend insisted that he had been misquoted but the newspaper stood by its reporter. Margaret would be 25 on August 21 that year and it was presumed that Townsend was making it known that he still loved her.

The royal family headed north to Balmoral in August, followed by the world's press. But August 21 came and went with no announcement. Townsend was himself in England for the Farnborough Air Show and was hounded by journalists. Eventually, he returned to Brussels with nothing resolved. The royal family failed to deal with the matter among themselves, the Queen Mother becoming upset when asked about it and the Queen was reluctant to explain to her sister the real situation.

THE GRAVITY OF THE SITUATION

The new Prime Minister Anthony Eden visited the Queen at Balmoral and the issue of Margaret's marriage was high on the agenda. For Eden it was a matter very close to home,

and possibly slightly embarrassing, as he had been the innocent party in a divorce and had then remarried. Even after Eden's visit, the royal family still failed to discuss the issue. Townsend was returning to London for three weeks in October and Elizabeth had agreed to allow her sister to see as much of him as she could to help her to come to a decision.

On October 11, as Margaret took a train south to see the man she loved, his picture was on the front page of every newspaper. They were reunited in London and embarked upon a series of dinner engagements with friends. Around this time, Lord Salisbury advised the royal family that it should make a public statement to short-circuit the constant media speculation.

On October 14, therefore, a statement was issued by press secretary Richard Colville. It insisted that "no announcement concerning Princess Margaret's immediate future was at present contemplated." It also asked that her privacy be respected, a request that had little chance of being observed and, indeed, reporters continued to follow the couple wherever they went. The Queen and Queen Mother were now aware of the gravity of the situation and the disastrous effect it was having on the monarchy.

THE DAMAGE DONE

On October 18, Eden traveled to Balmoral for his Tuesday audience bringing with him the news that the Cabinet's view remained unchanged. Furthermore, if the Princess went ahead and married Townsend, the Government would have no option but to introduce a bill in Parliament depriving her and any children she might have of the right of succession.

She would also lose her position as a Counsellor of State and her right to an income from the Civil List. It was also likely that the couple would have to live abroad, for a few years at least. More concerning, Eden advised the Queen, was how much the issue would undermine the image of the monarchy.

When Princess Margaret visited London's East End, she was greeted by shouts of support. "Go on Marge, do what you want," women called to her. Meanwhile, the popular press ranted about the hypocrisy of the establishment and the Church of England, and traditionalists railed against the horror of a princess marrying a man who had been through the divorce courts.

It has to be remembered that divorcees were *persona non grata* in royal palaces, on the royal yacht and on the royal lawn at Ascot. The Prime Minister was a divorced man himself as were two members of the Cabinet of the day. But the royal family was considered to be different, as *The Times* was at pains to point out:

> *... the Queen has come to be the symbol of everyday life of this society, its universal representative in whom her people see their better selves ideally reflected; and since part of their ideal is family life, the Queen's family has its own part in the reflection. If the marriage which is now being discussed comes to pass, it is inevitable that this reflection becomes distorted ...*

THE IMPOSSIBLE DREAM

Undoubtedly their hopeless situation was beginning to grow in the minds of the couple. The reality, too. They would have to get by on what Townsend earned and his income was already being eaten up by the education of his two sons. In the end, the decision not to marry was mutual.

By October 27, Margaret had made her intentions known to the Archbishop of Canterbury. They spent one final weekend together at the home of Lord Rupert Neville (1923 – 82) and met for a final time at Clarence House on the evening of Monday, October 31.

Princess Margaret issued a statement shortly after they parted for the final time that evening:

> *I would like it to be known that I have decided not to marry Group Captain Peter Townsend. I have been aware that, subject to renouncing my rights of succession, it might have been possible for me to contract a civil marriage. But, mindful of the Church's teaching that Christian marriage is indissoluble, and conscious of my duty to the Commonwealth, I have resolved to put these considerations before any others. I have reached this decision entirely alone, and in doing so I have been strengthened by the unfailing support and devotion of Group Captain Townsend. I am deeply grateful for the concern of all those who have constantly prayed for my happiness.*

It was signed simply "Margaret." The impossible dream was over.

A tearful Princess Margaret returns to Clarence House after a weekend in the country where Group Captain Peter Townsend was also a guest.

Anthony Eden

Robert Anthony Eden (1897 – 1977) was born at Windlestone Hall in County Durham, younger son of Sir William Eden, a Baronet, former colonel and local magistrate. He was educated at Eton and Christ Church College, Oxford. Before Oxford, however, he fought in the First World War with the King's Royal Rifle Corps. He was awarded the Military Cross and at the age of just 19 was the youngest adjutant on the Western Front. Before the end of the war, he became the youngest brigade-major in the British Army. After he left the army, he was elected to Parliament as MP for Warwick and Leamington at the age of 26.

Eden's first government post was as Under-Secretary for Foreign Affairs in Ramsay MacDonald's National Government. He was, as were many others who had fought in the Great War, vehemently anti-war and worked through the League of Nations to maintain peace. When he made a speech against Winston Churchill about the rearmament of Germany in the Commons—Churchill was against it—he was widely praised.

Neville Chamberlain said of him: "That young man is coming along rapidly; not only can he make a good speech but he has a good head and what advice he gives is listened to by the Cabinet." In 1933, he was appointed Lord Privy Seal. He became opposed to the appeasement of both Italy and Nazi Germany in the 1930s and was made Foreign Secretary in 1935. Mussolini called Eden "the best-dressed fool in Europe" and, indeed, Eden was always dapper. He dressed well and often wore a Homburg hat, a style that became known in Britain as an "Anthony Eden."

He resigned in 1938, increasingly unhappy with Chamberlain's policy of appeasement. He opposed the Munich Agreement, abstaining when the Commons voted on it. At the start of the Second World War, he was appointed Secretary of State for Dominion Affairs but was not in the War cabinet. When Churchill replaced Chamberlain as Prime Minister, he made Eden his Secretary of State for War before moving him back to the Foreign Office.

In 1945, when Labour came to power he was Deputy Leader of the Conservative Party, with many feeling that Churchill should retire and let Eden be Prime Minister. Then, when the Conservative Party returned to power in 1951, Eden was again appointed Foreign Secretary. He was knighted in 1954 and in April 1955 finally became Prime Minister when Churchill retired.

He immediately called a general election at which he increased the Conservative majority in the House of Commons. Eden resigned on January 9, 1957, following the Suez catastrophe and after doctors told him he was risking his life by continuing as Prime Minister. He became Earl of Avon in 1961 and died on January 14, 1977, at age 79.

PRINCE PHILIP AND THE THURSDAY CLUB

THE SUEZ CRISIS

Britain's humiliating adventure in Suez in 1956 was a disaster for Anthony Eden, the Prime Minister who had replaced Churchill, and would provide the Queen with another crisis.

Egyptian President Nasser nationalized the Suez Canal on July 26, closing it to Israeli ships. On October 29 that year, in a bid to take the canal back into western control, Israel, as part of a plan agreed with Britain and France, invaded the Egyptian Sinai and on November 5, British and French paratroopers landed along the canal. Egypt was defeated but blocked the waterway to shipping.

The United States refused to become involved and along with the Soviet Union applied pressure for the British, French, and Israelis to withdraw. President Eisenhower had already urged Britain not to invade and as a consequence of their ignoring his views, he threatened to seriously damage the British economy by selling The United States' Government's stock of sterling bonds. Meanwhile, the world and many in Britain were outraged by the action.

It was a moment of great consequence, probably signifying the end of Britain's role as a major global power and leading to the resignation of Anthony Eden. The Queen herself became a target for criticism. Many wanted to know how much she knew about the invasion beforehand and whether she had approved it.

The official papers that would tell us may have been destroyed and even if they have survived, there is a rule that prohibits royal-related material in the Whitehall archives being opened for a hundred years. Documents have surfaced, however, that suggest the Queen was heavily briefed sometimes twice daily on Suez between November 1 and 22, 1956.

THE WIND OF CHANGE

Former Guards officer Harold Macmillan (1894 – 1986) replaced Eden as Prime Minister on January 10, 1957. Macmillan was a complex man whom the Queen already knew, but the public was disappointed, having expected R.A. "Rab" Butler (1902 – 82) to be given the job. It was a difficult time, Britain having been relegated by the Suez disaster to the second division of world powers.

People believed that their world was being ruined by the outdated attitudes of the establishment which were stuck in the past and had little relevance to the modern world. The Suez crisis, the Peter Townsend affair, and the appointment of Harold Macmillan conspired to make the British people disillusioned. They felt their nation was governed by an elite that acted in its own interests and used the monarchy to support its dubious actions. There was a feeling that Britain's days of mattering were gone.

ANTI-ROYAL FEELING

Antipathy to the establishment and to the royal family increased. Playwright John Osborne (1929 – 94), riding the crest of a wave after the success of his play about working-class life,

Look Back in Anger, called it "a gold filling in a mouth full of decay." Writer and broadcaster Malcolm Muggeridge (1903 – 90) wrote in the *Saturday Evening Post* of "the Royal soap opera ... a sort of substitute or ersatz religion."

Other articles criticized the restricted nature of those around the Queen, "a tight little enclave of British ladies and gentlemen" as Lord Altrincham (1924 – 2001) put it in his magazine, the *National and English Review.* His sensational attack became personal, saying of the Queen:

> *Like her mother, she appears to be unable to string even a few sentences together without a written text ... The personality conveyed by the utterances which are put into her mouth is that of a priggish schoolgirl, captain of the hockey team, a prefect, and a recent candidate for Confirmation.*

Altrincham was physically attacked for these words and disowned by the town of Altrincham in Cheshire where his father had taken his hereditary title from. Lord Altrincham was simply tired of the sycophancy surrounding the Queen and the royal family and advocated the widening of the circle around them. His view was endorsed by a *Daily Mail* poll of readers between the ages of 16 and 34.

Sir Alan Lascelles retired in 1953 after the Coronation, refusing a peerage and other honors. He was replaced by Sir Michael Adeane, a man who was perfect for the job. He was bright, self-effacing and had a sense of humor, an essential element of survival at court. He represented continuity and, as such, was a traditionalist who was cautiously conservative in his approach to the job.

QUEEN ELIZABETH'S COURT

The organization that surrounded Queen Elizabeth was not much different to that which existed during her father's reign. Head of the household was the Lord Chamberlain to whom the heads of six departments reported. Among these were the Private Secretary whose job it was to deal with the monarch's official business; the Keeper of the Privy Purse, the treasurer for the Queen; and the Comptroller, who had responsibility for royal events such as weddings and funerals, garden parties, investitures, and visits by foreign dignitaries.

The office of the Lord Chamberlain was also at the time responsible for the various royal collections, books, paintings, and so on. Under the purlieu of the Lord Chancellor were also lords-in-waiting, gentlemen-at-arms, Yeomen of the Guard, the Royal Company of Archers, the Marshal of the Diplomatic Corps, the Secretary of the Central Chancery in charge of the various Orders.

The other departments were controlled by the Master of the Household—responsible for domestic arrangements and staff. This department also took care of horses, carriages, and cars. The Mistress of the Robes, who is usually a Duchess, is the most important of the ladies working for the Queen. The role is mainly honorary, although she does manage the rota of the Queen's ladies-in-waiting.

Under her are the Ladies of the Bedchamber, wives of peers who are with the Queen on tours and at important events but the everyday work is left to the Women of the Bedchamber, of whom there are four. These women, usually titled, deal with the Queen's private correspondence, do her shopping for gifts, make her private and official arrangements. Remunerated very little, although enjoying perks such as residence at royal palaces, these ladies are recruited on personal recommendation and personality.

One of the most important figures was Bobo MacDonald who was officially one of the Queen's two dressers, but she was allowed duties beyond that and even senior male officials of the royal household were afraid of her. "She had a great influence on the Queen ... a formidable lady," was how one courtier described her. "If the Queen said something and Miss MacDonald said something else—then it would probably go Bobo's way." She was said to be the only person in the Palace who could make the Queen cry, probably because Bobo had been around her since she was a baby.

LOSING MIKE PARKER

As British troops parachuted down beside the Suez Canal, the Duke of Edinburgh was halfway through a tour of outlying Commonwealth territories, accompanied by his Private Secretary, Commander Mike Parker. It was part of his trip to open the 1956 Olympic Games being staged in November 1956 in Melbourne, Australia.

Free of the restrictions of life at Buckingham Palace, Philip acted like he was back at sea on a Naval tour of duty. He grew a beard and visited the British scientific base in Antarctica. The break from his family inevitably led to some speculation that the royal marriage was in trouble, *Time* magazine reported in February 1957 that:

... the [rumor] mongering winds were howling louder around Buckingham Palace than they had since the days of Wallis Warfield Simpson and Edward VIII.

One marriage that was indeed in trouble however, was that of Mike Parker whose wife was suing him for divorce. The story broke in the press and Parker flew back from Gibraltar and immediately resigned to save Philip from being associated with anything nasty. As was evident from the Peter Townsend episode, divorce was still something Buckingham Palace wanted nothing to do with.

The *Daily Express* newspaper took Parker's side. The owner Lord Beaverbrook (1879 – 1964) was always happy to take a potshot at the royals in the pages of his newspaper. "Why should a broken marriage be a disqualification for royal service?" the *Daily Express* asked, mentioning Anthony Eden's divorce. But losing Mike Parker left a gap in Philip's life. He had enabled him to escape the stuffiness of Palace life. Parker had even learned to fly with him.

The bearded Duke of Edinburgh takes the tiller of the longboat "Lorna" when coming ashore from the royal yacht *Britannia* at Tristan da Cunha during his Commonwealth tour, January 1, 1957. Fred Swalos the coxswain of the boat watches nervously.

PRINCE PHILIP'S OTHER WOMEN

To the horror of the Palace, Philip was linked in the gossip columns to the actress and musical star Pat Kirkwood (1921 – 2007) whose legs the critic Kenneth Tynan (1927 – 80) had once labelled "the eighth wonder of the world." Philip had been introduced to her in 1948 in her dressing room at the London Hippodrome theater where she was performing. That evening they went to dinner at Les Ambassadeurs restaurant in Mayfair. They then danced together at Milroy's night club and reportedly had breakfast together the following morning. She recalled the Prince as "… so full of life and energy. I suspect he felt trapped and rarely got a chance to be himself. I think I got off on the right foot because I made him laugh."

When King George heard reports of their liaison, he is said to have been furious. Rumors persisted for many years about the couple although Kirkwood has always insisted that there was no affair. She and her husband actually approached Prince Philip's aide Brian McGrath, asking to be able to send a message to the Queen telling her that the persistent rumors were totally untrue.

There were also rumors of an affair with a Greek cabaret star in the late 1950s but they were denied. Philip always insisted it would be impossible for him to escape the attentions of his detectives long enough to indulge in such liaisons.

Other famous and beautiful women alleged to have been Philip's lovers over the years include the Countess of Westmoreland (1928 – 2009) who was married to the Queen's Master of Horse; actresses Merle Oberon (1911 – 79) and Anna Massey (1937 – 2011); television personality Katie Boyle (born 1926); Susan Barrantes (1937 – 98) the mother of the Duchess of York; the Duchess of Abercorn (born 1946) who is wife of the Lord Steward of the Royal Household; Princess Alexandra (born 1936) the Queen's cousin; and Lady Penny Brabourne (born 1953) his constant companion at carriage-driving events.

Actress Pat Kirkwood, October 1950.

THE THURSDAY CLUB

Despite Mike Parker's best efforts, Prince Philip became involved when reporters started to investigate Parker's past activities along with his own. They dug up a Private Members club that Parker and Philip both frequented, organized by the society photographer Baron (a.k.a. Stirling Nahum, 1906 – 56). The Thursday Club met in an upstairs room at Wheeler's Restaurant in London's Soho. Members included newspaper editors, and film stars like David Niven (1910 – 83) and Peter Ustinov (1921 – 2004).

But there were also less reputable club members such as Stephen Ward (1912 – 63), later notorious as one of the central figures in the Profumo Scandal, and the Soviet spy Kim Philby (1912 – 88). The club organized a bachelor party for Philip at Baron's flat and a dinner for the Prince was held every year at Mike Parker's flat.

After that Philip was no longer a regular attendee at the Thursday Club and was more likely to spend his leisure time sailing, a pastime he loved. He would go out in his Dragon-class yacht, *Bluebottle*, with his sailing companion, Uffa Fox (1898 – 1972), an English boat designer. He regularly attended the Cowes Week regatta and was a highly competitive sailor.

THE DUKE FINDS A ROLE

The Duke of Edinburgh was never made Prince Consort, as Queen Victoria had done with Prince Albert, and he saw no state papers but gradually he began to create a role for himself. He already ran the royal country estates but by 1956 he was finding other roles in areas that were of interest to him. He became Patron of the Industrial Society and President of the British Association for the Advancement of Science.

He supported young people as President of the National Playing Fields Association and Patron of the Outward Bound Trust. He was also President of the Central Council of Physical Recreation, the Amateur Athletics Board, the Commonwealth Games Association, and the Royal Yachting Association. With the founder of his old school, Gordonstoun, he established the Duke of Edinburgh Award Scheme which aimed to give young people the opportunity to stretch their minds, imagination and physical capabilities.

PRINCE OF THE UNITED KINGDOM

Philip's natural abrasiveness—some have called it arrogance—and inability to suffer fools, occasionally got him into trouble.

His relationship with the press was bad from the beginning. A courtier confessed that "the Duke is beginning to get journalists on his nerves ... and that [the Palace] is always afraid of some outburst." He threw nuts at cameramen in Gibraltar, "accidentally" turned a water hose on journalists at the Chelsea Flower Show, and when he saw a photographer climbing to try to get a better shot, the Prince told him he hoped he broke his neck.

The Queen took steps to mitigate the disappointment he felt at the outcome of the Mountbatten-Windsor naming issue. Among these was that she wished him to be Regent in the event of her death before Prince Charles turned 18. The Government hurriedly introduced a Regency Bill that had to be passed before the Queen left on her 1953 tour of the Commonwealth. This was taken as a direct snub to Princess Margaret because of the Peter Townsend affair. The Princess, according to the Regency Act of 1937, as the next in line of succession should act as regent.

On February 22, 1957, after it was suggested not by the Queen but by Winston Churchill, Philip was promoted to Prince of the United Kingdom. Churchill had first proposed it to Elizabeth in 1955 and although she was in favor she did nothing for the next two years to progress it. It was hoped that the Queen's reward to her husband for his service for the country might help to put an end to the rumors about the royal marriage falling apart.

Queen Elizabeth II with Prince Philip after their reunion at Lisbon on the royal visit to Portugal, February 1957.

CHAPTER 14

THE LITTLE BRITISH SOVEREIGN

In the spring and summer of 1957, Elizabeth and her husband were working happily together. There was a state visit to Portugal in February and the couple returned to Paris in April where they were once again rapturously received. October saw a visit to the United States to celebrate the 350th anniversary of the founding of the state of Virginia. Suez, it appeared, had made little difference to the high regard in which the British royal family were held.

More than a million people cheered them, along with President Dwight D. Eisenhower (1890 – 1969) and his wife Mamie (1896 – 1979) into Washington DC. They spent four nights at the White House, attending receptions and dinners, the news outlets describing her as "the little British sovereign."

She saw a game of American football, wearing a $43,000 mink coat that had been presented to her by a group of American fur farmers. She and Philip were then taken to visit a supermarket, the first they had ever seen.

Prime Minister Harold Macmillan had been anxious to repair the harm done by Suez to British-American relations. He was reassured when he was told by the British Ambassador Sir Harold Caccia (1905 – 90) that Elizabeth had "buried George III for good and all."

The Queen with US President Dwight D. Eisenhower at a White House State banquet, October 1957.

DISTANT AND FORMIDABLE

As ever the children did not travel with their parents. Prince Charles was often depicted as a lonely little boy. His clothes were anachronistic, bought from expensive Bond Street shops but more befitting the 1930s than the 1950s.

The people closest to him, as was the case with many upper-class children, were his nannies. Prince Philip had not been around for his first three birthdays and on his fifth in 1953, the young Prince spent the day at Windsor with his grandmother and Aunt Margaret.

That Christmas, the Queen and the Duke were in New Zealand and were away from November 23 until May 2. The Queen endeavored to spend an hour with her children in the morning and at bath-time, when she was able, but for the remainder of the day she was perfectly happy to let the nannies and governesses deal with them. One friend said "Motherhood is not the Queen's suit."

Philip has often been presented as a distant parent as well, but his children and people working in the Palace have said otherwise. According to Princess Anne, he tried to spend time with them before bedtime, and gave time to reading to them or playing with them. In fact some members of staff say it was Elizabeth who was more formidable.

She stuck very much to the royal rule that emotion is never shown in public, having been clearly instructed by her grandfather King George V at a very young age how to behave when she greeted her parents returning from a five-month tour of Australia: "We will not embrace at the station before so many people. When you kiss mama, take your hat off ..."

HIS MOTHER'S FOOTSTEPS

Charles was a sensitive child who responded badly to criticism or chiding, withdrawing into himself when that occurred. His sister Anne on the other hand, was much more confident, a boisterous child with a more outgoing personality. She was also quite naughty. Charles was taught at home by a governess, Miss Peebles, to begin with. His mother realized that he was not yet ready for the rough and tumble of the outside world.

Like his mother before him, he grew up in a world of adults and had little to do with children his own age. Also like his mother, he was taken on visits to museums and historic sites to broaden his knowledge. However these visits had to stop because of the interest shown in them by the media. The Queen wrote to newspaper editors asking for understanding but the frenzied press activity around the future king stopped for only a short time.

THE LONELY DAYS OF PRINCE CHARLES

At the end of January 1957, at the age of 8, he was finally sent to school, the first heir to the throne to attend primary school. He went to Hill House, located behind Harrods in Hans Place, one of the most exclusive parts of London. The school uniform was a mustard-colored sweater and rust-colored corduroy breeches. Founded by a former artillery officer with a sporting background, the school was not too academically competitive, its motto being "A boy's mind is not a vessel to be filled but a fire to be kindled."

It turned into a nightmare. All was fine the first day, but on the second everyone knew, and a crowd gathered of members of the public and photographers. On the third day, his mother decided to keep him home and asked Richard Colville to telephone newspaper editors asking them to desist.

Charles's next school, at the age of 9, was a boarding school, Cheam, a preparatory school in Hampshire, the school of choice for every Mountbatten male apart from Prince Philip. Charles had been dreading it and he later recalled those early days at the school as probably the loneliest of his life. The Queen had asked that he be treated like all the other boys, but, of course, that was difficult.

For the Prince, his lack of experience of life made it all the more difficult to become part of a group of boys or be accepted by his peers. It was patently obvious to everyone that he was very unhappy, but the Queen believed he would just have to get through it, that it would benefit him in his later role.

BECOMING THE PRINCE OF WALES

At the end of the summer term at Cheam, the Queen announced that she was going to make Charles the Prince of Wales, the traditional title accorded to heirs to the throne. She was incapacitated following an operation for sinusitis and so the news came as part of a prerecorded message at the opening of the Commonwealth Games in Cardiff:

I want to take this opportunity of speaking to all Welsh people, not only in this arena but wherever they may be. The British Empire and Commonwealth Games in the capital, together with all the activities of the Festival of Wales, have made this a memorable year for the principality. I have therefore decided to mark it further by an act which will, I hope, give as much pleasure to all Welshmen as it does to me. I intend to create my son, Charles, Prince of Wales today. When he is grown up I will present him to you at Caernarfon.

The 9-year-old Prince Charles found out about it as he watched television at Cheam with a bunch of other pupils. He had not been warned by anyone, least of all his mother and was deeply embarrassed by the news.

THE MOUNTBATTEN-WINDSOR CONNECTION

At the end of June 1959, the Queen arrived in Canada for a massive tour. Unknown to everyone, however, was the fact that she was pregnant with her third child. She covered 15,000 miles and opened the St. Lawrence Seaway. She sailed to Chicago on the royal yacht and received another warm welcome from the people of that city. Then she flew back to Britain where her pregnancy was made public. The family were joined on their annual holiday at Balmoral that year by President Eisenhower and his wife.

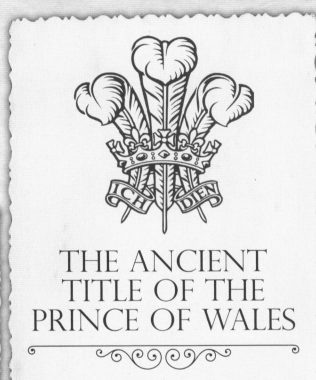

THE ANCIENT TITLE OF THE PRINCE OF WALES

The Prince of Wales is a traditional title given to princes born in Wales and dating back to the twelfth century. Before this, the most powerful Welsh ruler was usually known as King of the Britons but this evolved into Prince of Wales in the twelfth and thirteenth centuries. The first English person to be invested with the title was Edward (later Edward II, 1284 – 1327), son of the English King Edward I (1239 – 1307), in 1301 at Caernarfon where he was born. Since the time of Edward III, the title has been given to the heir apparent to the English and then the British throne. It is given as a personal honor or dignity and has no link with the right to succession. The title Earl of Chester has been given at the same time since 1399.

Apparently, the royal couple had been trying for a baby for several years and were delighted when Prince Andrew was born on February 19, 1960, named after Philip's grandfather. This may have been an effort by the Queen to please her husband but a few days prior to the baby's birth, she had done something else to please him. On February 8, she released a declaration made in Privy Council:

> *Now therefore I declare my Will and Pleasure ... while I and my children will continue to be styled and known as the House and Family of Windsor, my descendants, other than descendants enjoying the style, title or attributes of Royal Highness and the titular dignity of Prince or Princess, and female descendants who marry and their descendants, shall bear the name Mountbatten-Windsor ...*

The name Windsor would remain but more distant descendants would enjoy the name Mountbatten-Windsor, something of a symbolic gesture toward the Duke of Edinburgh.

Harold Macmillan claimed credit for this but it has been reported as an initiative devised by Martin Charteris. There had certainly been some lobbying from both Philip and Lord Mountbatten for the change but it was an idea that the Queen claimed was "very close to her heart."

The Cabinet was insistent that the name Windsor be retained for members of the Royal House, but, interestingly, when Princess Anne married Captain Mark Phillips in 1973, she was listed on the marriage register as "Mountbatten-Windsor," which was against what the 1960 statement had stipulated.

MARGARET STEALS THE HEADLINES

Princess Margaret's male friends had one-by-one got married, all except Billy Wallace (1927 – 77), the wealthy son of Captain Euan Wallace (1892 – 1941) who served briefly as Minister for Transport during the war. Wallace proposed to

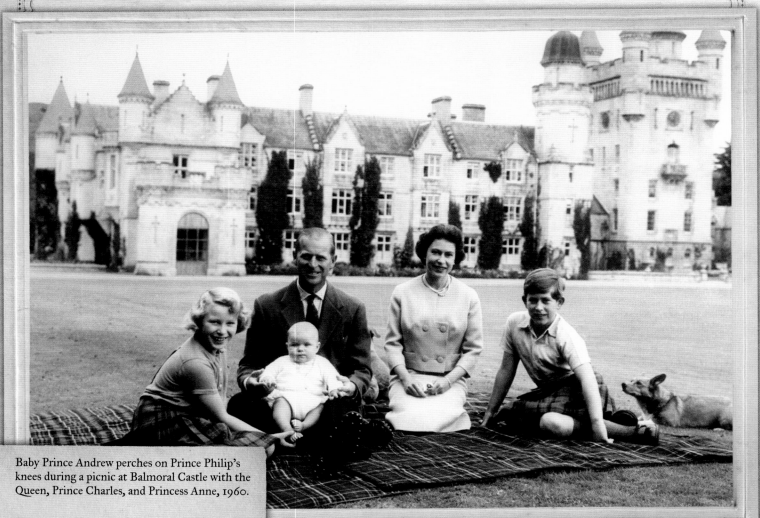

Baby Prince Andrew perches on Prince Philip's knees during a picnic at Balmoral Castle with the Queen, Prince Charles, and Princess Anne, 1960.

the Princess numerous times before she finally agreed to marry him, but the engagement floundered after Wallace enjoyed himself rather too much during a holiday in Barbados.

Since the Townsend affair, the Princess had become increasingly difficult and because the Queen felt responsible for the way Margaret's life had turned out, Elizabeth tended to indulge her. Sir Alan Lascelles confided in a friend, "Ever since the breach with Townsend, she has become selfish and hard and wild."

She was often rude to Elizabeth despite her seniority. One politician found her attitude toward the Queen to be "informal to the point of coarseness." Her resentment was noticed by the press when Elizabeth celebrated her tenth wedding anniversary by hosting a ball at the Palace. Margaret went out instead with friends and arrived back at the Palace around midnight, staying at the ball for less than an hour.

In March 1958, with the Queen Mother's indulgent permission, she had a rendezvous with Peter Townsend at Clarence House. The following day the meeting was splashed across the front pages, and the Queen who was in the middle of a state visit to the Netherlands was furious. Her own visit was relegated to the inside pages while Margaret stole the headlines.

She continued to see Townsend and once again the rumor mill ground out marriage speculation. The Palace firmly denied any notion of marriage and Margaret and Townsend went their separate ways once more. A year later, Townsend who was 44, married a 20-year-old Belgian woman who very closely resembled Princess Margaret.

THE PRINCESS AND THE PHOTOGRAPHER

By this time however, Princess Margaret was herself enamored of the young photographer Antony Armstrong-Jones (1930 – 2017). The couple met in the fall of 1958 at a dinner party at the home of one of Margaret's ladies-in-waiting, Lady Elizabeth Cavendish (born 1926).

Lady Elizabeth had invited Armstrong-Jones for a reason. She believed him to be just the type of young man who might shake Margaret out of the misery she had been experiencing since her break-up with Townsend. He was attractive, uninhibited, friendly, and relaxed and it became evident that the two were attracted to one another.

When the Queen Mother was introduced to him she liked him a great deal. He rented a room at Rotherhithe on the river Thames in southeast London where they met clandestinely. They also met at his photographic studio in Pimlico Road in south-west London. Margaret was having fun, relaxing in an informal way she had never experienced and enjoying the company of a more artistic, wilder group of friends.

He was invited to Balmoral by the Queen in 1959 and it all passed unnoticed by the media who believed he was around the royal family purely in his role of photographer. He and Margaret became privately engaged in December 1959 and in January 1960, Armstrong-Jones formally requested the Princess's hand in marriage.

The news was made public a week after the birth of Prince Andrew. There were those who were unhappy at the engagement of a princess to a lowly photographer and many European royals declined their invitation to the wedding for that very reason.

They were married at Westminster Abbey on May 6, 1960, in a lavish ceremony broadcast live around the world with a brilliant commentary by master broadcaster Richard Dimbleby (1913 – 65). The wedding cost £26,000 (around £550,000 in today's money) and questions were asked about the cost of their six-week honeymoon on *Britannia*. The Queen Mother tried to take the sting out of such complaints by announcing that she would pay for it. But at the end of the day the government paid up anyway.

Antony Armstrong-Jones, Lord Snowdon

Antony Charles Robert Armstrong-Jones, 1st Earl of Snowdon (1930 – 2017), was the son of a barrister, Ronald Armstrong-Jones (1899 – 1966) and his first wife, Anne Messel (1902 – 92) who went on to marry the 6th Earl of Rosse (1906 – 79). The couple separated when he was young.

While still at school, Antony contracted polio and during the six months he was in hospital, only his sister visited him and neither of his parents. He went to Eton and Jesus College, Cambridge, studying architecture but failing his exams in second year. He was the cox of the winning Cambridge boat in the Oxford vs. Cambridge Boat Race in 1950.

After he left university, he launched a career as a photographer, specializing in fashion, design, and theater and later took many royal portraits. In February 1960, he became engaged to the Queen's sister Princess Margaret, and they married on May 6, 1960, at Westminster Abbey. He was created Earl of Snowdon and Viscount Linley of Nymans in the County of Sussex on October 6, 1961.

Lord Snowdon as he was commonly known became the artistic advisor of *The Sunday Times Magazine* in the early 1960s and had established a reputation by the 1970s as one of Britain's most respected photographers. Many of his pictures appeared in the world's leading publications, such as *Vogue* and *Vanity Fair* and he photographed many of the best-known figures of his day.

In 1968, he made an award-winning documentary film, *Don't Count the Candles*, on the subject of aging. Several more followed. He co-designed the aviary at London Zoo and played a leading role in the organization of Prince Charles's investiture as Prince of Wales in 1969.

Lord Snowdon had many lovers, and his marriage to Princess Margaret eventually disintegrated, ending in divorce in 1978. They had two children, David, now the 2nd Earl of Snowdon (born 1961) and Lady Sarah Chatto (born 1964). He next married Lucy Lindsay-Hogg who became Countess of Snowdon, the former wife of the film director Michael Lindsay-Hogg (born 1940).

For twenty years from 1976 until 1996 he also had a mistress, the journalist Ann Hills who committed suicide in 1996. He and the Countess of Snowdon separated in 2000 after she learned that he had fathered a child, at the age of 67, with Melanie Cable-Alexander who was an editor at the magazine *Country Life*.

In 1999 Lord Snowdon was created Baron Armstrong-Jones of Nymans in the County of West Sussex. He died peacefully at his home in Kensington on January 13, 2017, at the age of 86.

CHAPTER 15

THE WIND OF CHANGE

Prime Minister Harold Macmillan began to look toward Europe as a possible way for Britain to maintain its position on the world stage as the 1950s turned into the 1960s. He also believed membership of the new Common Market might help Britain in its leadership of the Commonwealth.

The Queen could not do much to help in this but she did welcome General de Gaulle the President of France to Buckingham Palace on a very successful state visit. The General was still appreciative of the support he had received from George VI during the war and at a banquet he spoke emotionally about "the most precious encouragements the royal family had given him." The Queen also made a visit to Italy where she met the Pope at the Vatican.

TIGERS AND APARTHEID

In 1961, the Queen went to India and Africa. More than a million Indians welcomed her to New Delhi on the first visit by a monarch since that of her grandfather George V in 1911. As well as laying white roses at the tomb of the great assassinated Indian leader Mahatma Gandhi (1869 – 1948), she rode on a splendidly decorated ceremonial elephant in Jaipur.

Prince Philip controversially took part in a tiger hunt, bringing down a tiger with one shot. The news of his kill elicited outrage in Britain. The shooting of a female hippo by another member of the party, the Foreign Secretary Lord Home, brought further bad press.

The Commonwealth was shaken when South Africa voted in October 1960 to become a republic. Macmillan had flown there earlier in the year to make his famous "Wind of Change" speech, warning white South Africans that:

The wind of change is blowing through this continent. Whether we like it or not, this growth of national consciousness is a political fact.

Nonetheless, the South African Nationalist Government continued to pursue its policy of apartheid and the situation was a problem to Britain and the world for another three decades.

A DANGEROUS VISIT TO AFRICA

In November 1961, the Queen visited Ghana, a tour that had been postponed because of her pregnancy with Prince Andrew. Ghana had become a republic in July 1960, with Kwame Nkrumah (1909 – 72) as President. Nkrumah had become close to the Eastern Bloc and increasingly dictatorial. There was a concern that he might take Ghana out of the Commonwealth.

It was a dangerous visit with concerns for the wellbeing of Her Majesty in such a volatile country. Some thought it was wrong for the Queen to go because it gave credibility to an undemocratic regime. Debate raged in the press and in Parliament about the advisability of the tour and when bombs exploded in the Ghanaian capital Accra just a few days before the Queen's arrival, the Government seriously considered cancelling the trip, but it was decided to let it go ahead as planned.

Both Harold Macmillan and US President John F. Kennedy (1917 – 63) were determined to keep Ghana away from the clutches of the Soviets and the Queen's visit was seen as key to this objective, coupled with American funding for a dam on the Upper Volta. It was also a way for the British Government to stay close to America. As for the Queen, somewhat inevitably she insisted that she would go.

It went exceedingly well, and even the neo-Marxist Ghanaian newspaper, *The Evening News*, announced that it had been moved by this "most modest, lovable of Sovereigns." Unfortunately, however, the British press behaved in a less responsible manner, stirring up controversy with talk of limpet mines on *Britannia* and bomb plots.

So irritated was the Ghanaian government that they locked up the reporters from the *Daily Mail* and the *Daily Express* in jail. In order to board flights home, they had to be bailed out by the British High Commissioner to Ghana.

DENIED BY THE GENERAL

Ultimately, the Commonwealth was very concerned about Britain's attempts to join the Common Market. The Commonwealth leaders believed it could only be damaging to the organization. These feelings were made very clear at the September 1962 Commonwealth Conference in London. The Queen understood this and expressed her concern to her Prime Minister at their weekly meetings.

As it turned out, Britain was denied entry to Europe by General de Gaulle in early 1963. All Britain could do in response was peevishly cancel a visit to Paris by Princess Margaret and Antony Armstrong-Jones who had by this time been ennobled as the Earl of Snowdon.

STARTLED AND DISMAYED

On the streets of Britain, the Queen and the Duke of Edinburgh had the disturbing experience of being booed for the first time during a controversial state visit by Prince Philip's cousin, King Paul of the Hellenes (1901 – 64) and his wife Queen Frederica (1917 – 81).

The issue of Cyprus had put Britain and Greece at loggerheads and this visit was an effort to heal the wounds. Everyone knew that there would be demonstrations against the visiting King and Queen by left-wing protestors and the Greek Prime Minister had resigned after the King ignored his advice to cancel the visit.

Queen Frederica, a great-granddaughter of Queen Victoria, was the focus of the disquiet. She had strongly advocated the union of Cyprus with Greece and was often accused of extreme right-wing sympathies. She interfered in politics in Greece and was very outspoken.

The leader of the Labour opposition party Harold Wilson (1916 – 95) and his deputy George Brown (1914 – 85) refused to attend a state banquet for the visitors. Crowds of protesters had to be prevented from swarming

A grim evening for the British and Greek royal families after being booed when they attended a gala performance of *A Midsummer Night's Dream* at the Aldwych Theater, London, July 11, 1963.

up the Mall to Buckingham Palace where the banquet was being held.

At a special performance of *A Midsummer Night's Dream* the following night, as the royal party arrived and when they left, they were greeted by a chorus of boos and chants of the Nazi salute "Sieg heil!" "Startled and dismayed" was how one observer described the Queen at being greeted in such a manner.

SCANDALS UNRAVEL MACMILLAN

When the German President Theodor Heuss (1884 – 1963) visited London in 1958, he was given a particularly frosty welcome. The war was still fresh in people's memories. Elizabeth made a visit to Germany, the land of her ancestors, in 1965.

It was the first visit by a member of the British royal family to the country since before the First World War. For the Queen it was undoubtedly a difficult visit, because of the wars and the fact that some of her relatives had been Nazi functionaries. Ultimately, despite various familial complexities, the visit was a success.

By 1962, confidence in Harold Macmillan had reached rock-bottom and he had dismissed several of his Cabinet colleagues in what has become known as "The Night of the Long Knives." The fired ministers shared their feelings about the Prime Minister with the Queen in their farewell meetings with her.

In October, the Vassall Case added further concern about Macmillan. A homosexual civil servant John Vassall (1924 – 96) had been blackmailed by the Soviet Union into passing them secrets, and in 1963 two journalists were jailed for refusing to reveal their sources in the case. The press was up in arms.

In June of the same year, the Profumo scandal erupted. One of the names that came up in this scandal was Stephen Ward, an osteopath who was a member of the Thursday Club. Ward had actually drawn portraits of the Duke of Edinburgh and other members of the royal family that were hastily purchased by the Surveyor of the Queen's Pictures, Sir Anthony Blunt (1907 – 83), to save embarrassment.

There was also the scandal of the sensational divorce of the Duke (1903 – 73) and Duchess of Argyll (1912 – 93) that involved Conservative ministers. Macmillan was appalled by other people's lax morals and coped very badly with all of these cases. He wrote to the Queen:

I had, of course, no idea, of the strange underworld in which other people, alas, besides Mr. Profumo, have allowed themselves to be trapped.

ONE OF THEIR OWN

In October 1963, Harold Macmillan was taken ill and resigned as Prime Minister. Lord Home was chosen to succeed him. Lord Home's selection as leader lay in the hands of eight or nine Tory "grandees" and they selected, in effect, one of their own.

It was the Queen's prerogative to choose the Prime Minister but it was felt—and expressed by such politicians as Enoch Powell—that she had been left little option by Macmillan and the Tory hierarchy but to appoint Lord Home, leaving something of a bad taste at the end of Macmillan's premiership.

This was not helped by the fact that the new prime minister was an old family friend of the Queen Mother's. It gave the appearance of the establishment taking care of itself. The country had had no say in their new leader and essentially they had been given another Macmillan.

Lord Home was criticized relentlessly by the Labour Party as an aristocrat, out of touch with the problems of ordinary families, and he came over stiffly in television interviews, in contrast to the Labour leader Harold Wilson. Throughout his brief stay at 10 Downing Street, Lord Home's starchy demeanor and clipped upper class tones did not waver. He remained aristocratic and old-fashioned. The country knew it was time for a change.

THE PROFUMO AFFAIR

In 1963 the Macmillan Government was rocked by the political scandal surrounding John Profumo, the British Secretary of War. Profumo had been appointed to his post in 1960 by Harold Macmillan. It was a junior Cabinet position but Profumo seemed destined for great things. He was married to retired film star Valerie Hobson (1917 – 98).

In July 1961, he was introduced to 19-year-old model and showgirl Christine Keeler at a party at Cliveden, an estate belonging to Lord "Bill" Astor, an English businessman and Conservative politician. Keeler was at Cliveden as the guest of a society osteopath and Thursday Club member Stephen Ward.

Ward had also introduced her to Yevgeny Ivanov, a naval attaché at the Soviet embassy. Ivanov was an intelligence officer in the GRU, the Russian Main Intelligence Directorate, and Keeler was having a sexual relationship with him. She also began a brief affair with Profumo at the same time.

After an incident involving an ex-lover at Stephen Ward's apartment, the press began to get wind of Profumo's affair with Keeler. The issue was raised in the House of Commons on March 21, 1963, as a matter of national security because of the Ivanov connection, although British intelligence had already established that Profumo had not revealed any secrets.

Forced to make a statement, Profumo denied the allegations saying "There was no impropriety whatsoever in my acquaintanceship with Miss Keeler." He threatened to sue for slander if the accusations were repeated outside the House of Commons.

When Stephen Ward went on trial in May for prostituting Keeler and others, Keeler testified under oath about her relationship with Profumo. Meanwhile, Ward wrote to the opposition Labour leader Harold Wilson maintaining that Profumo had lied to the House. Profumo confessed and resigned his Cabinet position on June 5.

Harold Macmillan was the subject of much criticism for his handling of the matter. The young pop group The Beatles were lifting the country's spirits at the time and Macmillan was perceived as old and out-of-touch and even incompetent.

Macmillan resigned in October 1963 and the Conservatives lost the 1964 general election to Labour. Stephen Ward committed suicide, Christine Keeler went to prison for perjury, and Profumo devoted the remainder of his life to charitable work in London's East End.

Osteopath Stephen Ward with model Christine Keeler.

John Profumo, British Minister of War.

Sir Anthony Blunt

Anthony Frederick Blunt (1907 – 83) was a leading British art historian who began lecturing at the University of London in 1933. He was appointed to the distinguished position of Surveyor of the King's Pictures in 1945, and two years later became both Professor of the History of Art at the University of London, and the director of the Courtauld Institute of Art.

After the King's death in 1952 he became Surveyor of the Queen's Pictures and was in charge of the Royal Collection, one of the largest and richest collections of art in the world. He was knighted in 1956 for his work and became known as Sir Anthony Blunt. He was a third cousin to Queen Elizabeth the Queen Mother.

In 1964 he confessed to being a Soviet agent after he was discovered to be the legendary "Fourth Man" in the Cambridge spy ring. At the time he was given immunity from prosecution by the British intelligence services, partly because revealing his name would be deeply embarrassing and very damaging to the royal family. His confession was a closely held secret for many years and was only revealed publicly by Margaret Thatcher in 1979, when he was immediately stripped of his knighthood by the Queen.

But it seems like some Palace insiders may have known of Blunt's connections long before his public exposure. In 1948 Mr. Philip Hay attended an interview with Sir Alan Lascelles at Buckingham Palace for the post of private secretary to the Duchess of Kent. They happened to pass Blunt in a corridor and Lascelles whispered to Hay: "That's our Russian spy."

In his unfinished memoirs Blunt, who ended a broken man, conceded that spying for the Soviet Union was the biggest mistake of his life. He died of a heart attack at his London home in 1983 at the age of 75.

A TASTE OF NORMAL LIFE

When the Labour party won the 1964 election Home's replacement was Harold Wilson, a departure from recent Prime Ministers, in that he had enjoyed a provincial, middle-class upbringing in Yorkshire. He had gone to Oxford University and done very well there, but he remained close to his Yorkshire roots.

Wilson invariably smoked a pipe, even at the weekly audiences with the Queen. When he turned up for his first meeting with Her Majesty to "kiss hands" and receive his seals of office, he arrived with his father, his wife and two sons, and his private secretary Marcia Williams (born 1932).

Events did not go too well for Wilson at his first Tuesday meeting at the Palace with the Queen. She demonstrated how well prepared she was for such meetings by catching him inadequately briefed on an issue. It never happened again. But soon the two were getting on well, the Queen enjoying his relaxed attitude and his wit.

Wilson's audiences with the Queen gradually increased in length. He was even asked to stay for drinks on occasion, something that never happened. It was an education for her, learning about his provincial upbringing, about Labour philosophy, and the way trade unions worked.

Wilson managed to bring her a taste of the normal everyday life of the British people, something which the aristocratic politicians of recent times could never hope to do. He in turn grew to be very fond of her. This, according to some observers, blinded him to the normal processes. When an increase in the Civil List payments was on the table in 1975, Wilson agreed it without even putting it to Cabinet.

IMPARTIAL AND APOLITICAL

The Queen throughout her long reign has had to change and adapt to many different prime ministers and governments, although it has been said that she has always got on better with Labour ones than Conservatives.

It was rumored that senior British aristocrats looked down somewhat on the royal family which might also go some way to explaining why she got on better with politicians like Wilson. But, of course, she had to be seen to remain totally impartial and apolitical.

The left-wing Labour politician Richard Crossman (1907 – 74) wrote about the relationship between his colleagues and the Queen:

> *Barbara [Castle], Roy [Jenkins] and I are republicans. We don't like the royal position, we don't like going to Court or feel comfortable there, and we know the Queen isn't comfortable with us. Fred Peart, on the other hand, gets on with the Queen just like George Brown and Callaghan do ... Harold is a steady loyalist and, roughly speaking, it is true that it is the professional classes who in this sense are radical and the working-class socialists who are by and large staunchly monarchist. The nearer the Queen they get the more the working-class members of Cabinet love her and she loves them ...*

Crossman also objected strongly to Privy Council meetings being held wherever the Queen was. So, if she was on holiday at Balmoral, four Ministers of the Crown had to fly to Scotland for what was effectively two and a half minutes' work.

THE NATION'S GREATEST SUBJECT

On March 10, 1964, the Queen had her fourth and last child, Prince Edward. "Goodness what fun it is to have a baby in the house again!" she told one of her friends. It was interesting that although Charles when younger insisted that he was happiest when he was with his family, he later complained to his biographer Jonathan Dimbleby (born 1944) about his mother's remoteness and his father's rigid discipline, insisting that she seemed much more relaxed with his two youngest siblings. Her favorite son, apparently, was Andrew who made her want to be more involved with her children.

But there was sadness across the nation the following year when Winston Churchill passed away, at age 90, two weeks after suffering a massive stroke. Elizabeth insisted on a state funeral for the man to whom the nation owed so much and who had been so close to her father. More than 300,000 people filed past his coffin during his lying in state at Westminster Hall.

His funeral was a day on which the Queen ignored precedence and arrived at St. Paul's Cathedral to await her "greatest subject." She also permitted the Churchill family and the great man's coffin to leave the cathedral in front of her. The wreath she sent carried her funeral tribute: "From the Nation and the Commonwealth. In grateful remembrance. Elizabeth R."

RATTLE YOUR JEWELRY

It was also a time of change in attitudes toward the monarchy. The Queen's tenth anniversary on the throne passed without much notice being paid. Perhaps it was the case, as the journalist Malcolm Muggeridge told an American chat-show host, that "The English are getting bored with their monarchy."

The royal family were certainly not shown nearly as much deference as they had been in the past. When the Beatles strode onstage at London's Prince of Wales Theater for the Royal Variety Performance in front of the Queen Mother and Princess Margaret, the evening's best moment of entertainment wasn't one of the songs. Before closing with a rousing version of "Twist and Shout," John Lennon aimed one of the most infamous bits of stage banter in music history at the royal box:

For our last number, I'd like to ask your help. Will the people in the cheaper seats clap your hands? And for the rest of you, if you'll just rattle your jewelry ...

Princess Margaret was a huge Beatles fan, and she obviously had a lot of fun meeting them at the premier of their new movie *A Hard Day's Night* in July 1964. From left to right: Ringo Starr, Paul McCartney, John Lennon, and George Harrison, and a very happy Princess Margaret.

PART FOUR

ALL THAT GLITTERS IS NOT GOLD

No one who knew Diana will ever forget her.
Millions of others who never met her, but felt
that they knew her, will remember her.

Queen Elizabeth II

CHAPTER 16

THE FUTURE KING SWEARS ALLEGIANCE

Not far from Buckingham Palace, in the boutiques and clubs of King's Road in the fashionable Chelsea district of London, the Swinging Sixties and Beatlemania were beginning to change the world. What was happening outside never quite penetrated the walls of the Palace, however. But the royal children did feel the full force of the changes in morality and society in general.

The Queen and Prince Philip were deeply aware of their responsibility to bring up the heir to the throne so that when his turn came he would be up to the burden that the role inevitably brings. But, Charles was a sensitive, shy child and was even prone to self-pity. He was not at all athletic or likely to want to engage in the rough and tumble children normally enjoyed.

The women who surrounded him in his daily life—the Queen Mother, his nanny Mabel Anderson (born 1927), and his mother's lady-in-waiting Susan Hussey (born 1939)—adored him precisely for his nature. The Queen Mother saw some of her late husband's qualities in him.

The women encouraged his appreciation of music, art, and books, while his father on the other hand was impatient with him, even bullying him at times to the point of tears because he was not the type of son he wanted. His mother did not step in to defend him, probably because she agreed with her husband that Charles needed to "man up."

PUNCHING THE FUTURE KING

Inevitably, when it came to selecting a school for the Prince, Gordonstoun in Scotland was chosen as it was believed that it would "make a man of him." The Mountbattens were very keen for him to go there and Prince Philip had been a student there. This was against the wishes of the Queen Mother who believed that Eton would be altogether more appropriate for a boy of Charles's temperament, but she lost that particular argument.

On May 1, 1962, Charles flew north to Scotland, in a plane of the Queen's flight piloted by his father. He was extremely nervous

Prince Philip and Prince Charles being shown around the Gordonstoun grounds by Iain Tennant, May 1962.

and although three of his cousins—Prince Welf Ernst of Hanover (1947 – 81), Prince Alexander of Yugoslavia (born 1945), and Norton Knatchbull (born 1947) grandson of Lord Mountbatten—were also there, he still had a torrid time.

He was a victim of bullying, his large ears being a particular target. He was deeply lonely as no other boy wanted to get close to him for fear of being accused of ingratiating himself into the favors of the heir to the throne. It became a badge of honor to have a go at him, as the writer William Boyd who was there at the same time, witnessed:

> We did him over. We just punched the future King of England.

The spartan living conditions did not help. Charles was in Windmill Lodge, a stone and timber building in which there were fourteen boys to a dormitory on hard, wooden beds with naked lightbulbs and bare floorboards. The windows were left resolutely open every night, even during the coldest of Scottish winter nights.

It inevitably had the desired effect, toughening him up and making him more resilient but he hated his time there which was leavened only by trips to visit "Granny" at Birkhall and the local countryside and nearby sea. He begged her to persuade his parents to take him away from Gordonstoun but she refused. And, anyway, it would have been very embarrassing for all concerned.

COMING OUT OF HIDING

Even at that distance from London, the newspaper photographers still hounded him. On one famous occasion he fled the crowds who were following him, escaping into the confines of a local pub.

When he was asked what he would like to drink, the only drink he could think of was cherry brandy. He was just 14 years of age and it was illegal for him to drink alcohol. The story

hit the headlines and he was humiliated. As a result, his detective was withdrawn from royal duty which was also upsetting for him.

For three years, Charles had to put up with Gordonstoun, but in 1965, at the age of 17, he was sent to Timbertop, a school in Australia, for six months. He was accompanied by 35-year-old Squadron Leader David Checketts (born 1930) who would be by his side for the next 13 years, and as his private secretary from 1970 to 1978.

Living not far from the school, Checketts and his family provided a secure environment for the Prince at weekends but he was also adept at handling the press. He encouraged Charles to confront his responsibilities and come out of hiding. People were curious to see him, and Checketts persuaded him to go out and meet the public.

NOT A WORD OF WELSH

Charles's time in Australia turned out to be much more enjoyable than the grim first three years at Gordonstoun. He returned there and was appointed "Guardian" (head boy) of the school. When he left three terms later, he had the qualifications for entry to Trinity College, Cambridge, but had made not one lasting friendship in all his time there. He went back to the Palace even more withdrawn than before, to the disappointment of his mother and father.

The date for Charles's investiture as Prince of Wales had been set as July 1969 at Caernarfon Castle in north-west Wales, but it was realized as the date approached that he was something of a stranger to the country. This added fuel to the fire for Welsh Nationalists who were appalled at the idea of an English Prince of Wales. Charles had never lived in the country and spoke not a word of Welsh. The Queen decided, therefore, to transfer him from Cambridge University to the University of Aberystwyth on the west coast of Wales where he studied Welsh. At Cambridge he had been studying anthropology and archaeology.

THE FAMILY FEUD RUMBLES ON

The Duke and Duchess of Windsor had been living in Paris but Elizabeth demonstrated her family loyalty by making efforts at reconciliation throughout the 1960s. It was a delicate matter as she could not be seen to be in any way accepting of the Duke's actions as the Queen Mother was still very bitter toward him.

There was no doubt that the supposed feud between the two sides of the family was doing the image of the royal family no good. In fact, there was a poll in the *Daily Express* in 1962—the former King's twenty-fifth wedding anniversary—that showed a large percentage supportive of the Duke and Duchess being allowed to live in England once again.

Money had played a part in the cooling of relations. When the Queen withdrew the Duke's annual £10,000 allowance gifted by his brother George VI, he had understandably been incandescent. For their part, the Queen and her side were irritated by the stream of magazine and newspaper articles in which the Duke and Duchess tried to put their side of the story. At the same time the Duke needed to earn some money to fund their extravagant lifestyle.

In 1951, the Duke's memoirs—*A King's Story*—were published while King George VI was still alive but very sick. It was unpleasant to have the Abdication brought up yet again. Nonetheless, the book was a bestseller. So was Mrs. Simpson's autobiography *The Heart Has Its Reasons,* which was published five years later.

The royal family was disdainful of such books, believing it to be undignified and beneath them. They also still had bad memories of the treachery, of Crawfie's book in 1950.

THE DUKE'S NAZI CONNECTIONS

Worse for the Duke however, was the release of Nazi documents which showed that Hitler believed in the event of a German success in the war, the Duke was so bitter about his treatment that he could be persuaded to replace his brother on the British throne. There was no evidence to prove that this would actually have been the case but it was just another irritation to the Queen provided by "Uncle David" as the Duke was known to the family.

There was also trouble over an official biography of the late George VI by Sir John Wheeler-Bennett (1902 – 75). The Duke was concerned about what was going to be said about him and wanted to see it before publication but the Queen, who had commissioned the book, told him she would decide who would read it in advance. He was deeply offended and wrote to his lawyer:

> *I am incensed over this latest display of rudeness toward me from the palace, and am determined that, unless my niece has the common courtesy to give me an opportunity of reading all references to me in Wheeler-Bennett's official biography of my late brother, then no mention of me whatsoever shall appear therein.*

HEALING THE WOUNDS

The ensuing threat of legal action persuaded Elizabeth to let the Duke have sight of the appropriate sections of text. But the book was at pains not to make too much of the Abdication and the Duchess of Windsor was rarely referred to. The row over whether she should enjoy the title HRH, which had been the cause of so much division between family was hardly mentioned.

The Queen made strenuous efforts not to have any encounters with the Duke, having not seen him since 1953, and being deliberately absent when he was granted access to the archives at Windsor Castle for a book. This may have been partly because she was aware of black market currency dealings in which he had been involved. A scandal about such a matter would have been unbelievably damaging to the Crown.

When the Duke was in London for an eye operation in March 1965, she went to visit him at the London Clinic. There she encountered the Duchess of Windsor, probably for the first time since 1936, a meeting described by a spokesperson as "very private but very pleasant indeed." During this visit, she got to know her uncle a little better.

The Duke and Duchess joined the royal family for the first time at an official ceremony when a memorial plaque was unveiled to the memory of Queen Mary on the wall of Marlborough House. The talk was of whether the Duchess would curtsy to Elizabeth and she failed to do so. Pointedly, the Windsors were not invited to lunch with the royal family after the ceremony, eating instead with Princess Marina at Kensington Palace.

AGREEING TO DISAGREE

At the funeral of Princess Marina in 1968, the Duke attended on his own but during this visit, he obtained the permission of his niece for he and his wife to be buried in the royal family plot at Frogmore. He also negotiated that the £10,000 he received annually for his life interest in Sandringham and Balmoral would continue to be paid to his wife in the event of his death.

It took Elizabeth almost six months to give him a decision and even then, she told him it would be £5,000. Given what had passed and the ill-feeling that had existed, it can be viewed as a decent gesture, especially as the Duchess would hardly be poverty-stricken when her husband died.

The investiture of Prince Charles as Prince of Wales gave occasion for another attempt at reconciliation but the informal invitation the Queen sent did not extend to the Duchess of Windsor. Although the Abdication was now very distant from the younger members of the royal family, the Queen Mother still looked upon the Duchess as "the lowest of the low." In his response, the Duke was generous, making it easier for his niece:

As I do not believe the presence of his aged great-uncle would add much to the colorful proceedings centered upon Charles, I do not feel that I should accept. At the same time, I do appreciate your nice thoughts.

He was a little more irritated by the exclusion of the Duchess a few weeks later when he was invited to the dedication of the King George VI Memorial Chapel in St. George's, Windsor. He declined the invitation because he would be en route for the United States, but added:

Although you did not include Wallis by name on the invitation, I presume that you expected her to accompany me.

THE INVESTITURE OF THE PRINCE OF WALES

By the time the investiture took place at Caernarfon Castle on July 1, 1969, the atmosphere in Wales had changed considerably since the announcement twelve years before that Charles was to be Prince of Wales. The Welsh Nationalist movement, Plaid Cymru, had become more prominent and bombs had even been planted at Welsh public buildings.

The Queen informed Prime Minister Harold Wilson that she was afraid for the safety of her son. Charles was now actually living in Wales attending university at Aberystwyth, but to withdraw him would be embarrassing and would only heighten anti-English sentiment.

The security services mounted a large-scale operation in Aberystwyth to keep the Prince safe, with around seventy officers billeted there and operatives disguised as students and cleaners. It took considerable courage for Charles to persevere with his studies.

A bomb blew up a nearby RAF radio station and someone even tried to saw the head off a statue of the last Prince of Wales that stood on the town's promenade. The last Prince of Wales had been the Duke of Windsor.

BOMBS AND EXPLOSIONS

Unlike his predecessor, Prince Charles took the investiture very seriously. The ceremony was organized by the Duke of Norfolk and Lord Snowdon. Norfolk took care of the ceremonial details while Snowdon who had been appointed Constable of Caernarfon by Elizabeth in 1963, was in charge of the design. There was a modern Perspex canopy beneath which stood thrones made of Welsh slate for the Queen, Prince Philip, and Prince Charles.

Charles wore a military uniform and added some drama during the ceremony by donning a purple surcoat trimmed with ermine. Snowdon had argued for a very simple band of gold to serve as a coronet, a tribute to the princely appearance of old. But the crown used in the end was a modern version of the traditional Prince of Wales's coronet, complete with the requisite jewels, crosses, and fleur-de-lys.

There were the usual complaints about the money being spent on the investiture and many Welsh people opposed the whole idea. Bombs exploded on the eve of the ceremony as well as on the actual day. The royal train was even stopped by a bomb warning that turned out to be a hoax.

Two men died when a bomb they were planting near Caernarfon went off too soon. There was even an audible explosion as Charles's carriage made its way, carrying the Prince, the Welsh Secretary, and David Checketts along the route to Caernarfon Castle.

THE CEREMONY AT CAERNARFON

The ceremony started with Lord Snowdon as Constable of Caernarfon handing the Queen, dressed in a yellow outfit designed by Norman Hartnell, a key which she then returned to him. She made her way to her throne and the Prince's procession, including six Welsh peers carrying his insignia of office, arrived.

The insignia included a sword that had been used by George V as Prince of Wales, a golden scepter, a gold ring, the velvet mantle, and the coronet. The Home Secretary James Callaghan

The Queen and Prince Charles during the Investiture of the Prince of Wales at Caernarfon Castle, July 1969.

(1912 – 2005) read from the Letters Patent granting the Prince his title. He was then given his insignia and knelt in homage to Her Majesty, swearing:

> *I, Charles, Prince of Wales, do become your liege man of life and limb and of earthly worship, and faith and truth I will bear unto you to live and die against all manner of folks.*

The Queen placed the coronet on his head and the Prince of Wales reached up to gingerly secure it in place.

The previous investiture ceremony in 1911 had been to help Edward VII in his relationship with the difficult Welsh politician Lloyd George (1863 – 1945) who was Chancellor of the Exchequer at the time. This time it was to revive the royal family and the monarchy, but the seriousness with which the Queen and the young Prince approached it lent another dimension to the proceedings.

ROYAL FAMILY ON TELEVISION

The idea of a television documentary looking at the royal family as it went about its business was suggested. The Queen's advisors were worried that the royals were becoming distanced from their subjects and in an age of mass media and social change, they were seen as outdated and stuffy. The Queen was initially reluctant but was persuaded by Lord Mountbatten's family. Mountbatten was an inveterate seeker of publicity and his son-in-law, Lord Brabourne, was a successful film producer. Prince Philip was supportive of the idea.

One change in Palace staff helped the idea gain traction. In 1968 Commander Richard Colville retired and a young Australian William Heseltine (born 1930) arrived in the Palace Press Office. Heseltine had a much more accommodating attitude toward the press and was excited by the television show, especially as it was to be shown around the time of the investiture.

The series was phenomenally successful, being repeated five times in the following eighteen months. In Britain alone, it attracted an audience during these showings of around 40 million viewers. Although Elizabeth appeared relaxed and witty among her family and friends, Charles emerged as a rather serious, conventional and old-fashioned young man, nothing like the trendy youngsters on Britain's high streets. The Queen was seen at work, assembling outfits for tours with the trusty Bobo MacDonald and editing speeches with Sir Michael Adeane.

A ROYAL MAKEOVER

Audiences and ambassadorial receptions were filmed, the procedure for handing credentials to the Queen being explained to men such as Walter Annenberg, the millionaire US ambassador. Lunch with her husband was filmed and a royal garden party, the Queen smiling serenely throughout as if she was genuinely having a good time.

She was seen driving a Land Rover with the 5-year-old Prince Edward as her passenger at Sandringham and a royal barbecue was shown, Philip and Anne in charge of the cooking. The family were shown relaxing on *Britannia* which was obviously something of a retreat for them. At the end, the Queen, Philip, Charles, and Anne sat around a lunch table telling stories about their family.

The film, although hugely successful, brought warnings of what was to come, as the television critic Milton Schumann said:

> *... is it, in the long run, wise for the Queen's advisors to set as a precedent this right of the television camera to act as an image-making apparatus for the monarchy? Every institution that has so far attempted to use TV to popularize or aggrandize itself has been trivialized by it.*

CHAPTER 17

THE WEALTHIEST WOMAN IN THE WORLD

Prince Philip himself calls the blunders that he has made "dontopedalogy"—meaning putting one's foot in one's mouth. One of the worst examples of this occurred in 1969 during an interview for the American television program *Meet the Press*, when he said:

> *We go into the red next year, now, if nothing happens we shall either have to—I don't know, we may have to move into smaller premises, who knows? We've closed down—well, for instance we had a small yacht which we had to sell, and I shall probably have to give up polo fairly soon, things like that …*

There was understandable uproar. The Palace and the Government, who had already been involved in the always delicate negotiations about the Civil List, were appalled as they would far rather the matter had been kept as quiet as possible.

THE RICH LIST PROBLEM

But he was only telling the truth. In 1952, when the Queen acceded to the throne, the Civil List payment was set at £475,000 a year and this was no longer enough to pay for everything. The manner in which the Prince said it, and the flippant way he talked of having to give up polo, caused embarrassment for the Palace and Government.

There was huge indignation among the British public who treated Philip's outburst as incredible, given that his wife was reportedly one of the wealthiest women in the world. The problem was that the lists of the world's wealthiest people that were published counted into her wealth the royal palaces, the paintings, and the other *objets d'art* that she could never sell and which generated no income.

Harold Wilson announced that a Select Committee would be appointed to investigate the matter of royal finances at the start of the next Parliament, but Wilson's Labour Party lost the June 1970 general election and it was now up to Edward Heath (1916 – 2005), the new Conservative Prime Minister.

THE PRIVY PURSE

The Palace expenditure had been bolstered by contingency funds until 1970 when a mere £30,000 was left in reserve, leaving the Privy Purse to fund the deficit. The Privy Purse is the monarch's private income, mostly derived from the Duchy of Lancaster. By the end of 1971, it had to find £600,000. Lord Mountbatten pleaded with the Palace to be clear about the state of the monarch's finances with an article in the *Times*.

A few days later, Jock Colville who was now working for a bank wrote in the *Times* that the Queen was actually only worth about £12 million. This, however, did not stop the rich lists from still including palaces and collections in the estimation of her wealth.

The Select Committee brought more bad news. The Government, it seemed, was carrying many additional costs for the royal family that were not being paid for out of either the Civil List or the Privy Purse. To make matters worse, increases were being sought for the other members of the royal family.

It was claimed on their behalf that they shared the royal duties and that their relationship to the Queen and these duties made it impossible for them to take jobs. It was also pointed out, however, that the Queen had made contributions to the expenses of other members of the family.

A RANCOROUS DEBATE

Radical proposals were discussed in which everyone suffered. Elizabeth would be paid an annual salary of £100,000; the annual payment to the Queen Mother should be reduced to the equivalent of a Prime Minister's pension; Prince Philip's payment should be reduced to £20,000 a year from £40,000 and his household—separate to his wife's—would be abolished.

The annuities of Princess Margaret and the Duke of Gloucester were to be abolished; and the Queen would have to pay other members of her family out of her £100,000. Furthermore, the Prince of Wales was to be given a salary equal to that of the Prime Minister and he would be deprived of the income from the Duchy of Cornwall.

In the Commons, however, these ideas were voted down by the Conservative majority. In 1972, the Queen's Civil List payment was increased from £475,000 to £980,000 and there were equivalent increases for the rest of the royal family.

In 1975, the Labour Government set out that the Civil List should maintain its value in real terms every year. A rancorous debate in the Commons ensued with the Queen's immunity from taxation being dragged out once more.

REASSURING THE COMMONWEALTH

Britain entered the EEC on January 1, 1973, and the Queen had to spend several years on foreign tours to the countries of the Commonwealth, reassuring them that their interests were still paramount to Great Britain despite this new relationship with Europe.

Questions were asked in Canada, for instance, as to whether it was time for the country to have its own head of state.

During a short six-day trip to Australia in 1973 she gave her assent to the Royal Styles and Titles Bill which stipulated that when she was visiting Australia, the Queen would have the title "Queen of Australia," rather than "Queen

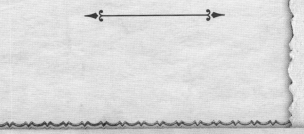

Looking like a million dollars, one of the wealthiest women in the world, Queen Elizabeth II wears the Grand Duchess Vladimir tiara of diamonds and pearls with the Queen Victoria Golden Jubilee necklace, 1976.

of the United Kingdom and Her Other Realms and Territories."

There was also a great deal of controversy about Britain's and the Queen's relationship with Australia in 1975 when the Queen's representative, Governor-General Sir John Kerr (1914 – 91), created a constitutional crisis by dismissing the Prime Minister, Gough Whitlam (1916 – 2014).

PRESERVING THE ROYAL FAMILY

When Harold Wilson returned to 10 Downing Street in 1974, he was not the energetic figure he had been in his first stint as Prime Minister and he informed the Queen that he was retiring from politics when he reached 60 in 1976. The Queen and Prince Philip attended his retirement dinner on April 5 that year.

It was the first time she had been inside the Prime Minister's residence since the retirement dinner of Winston Churchill twenty-one years previously. Wilson was succeeded by James "Jim" Callaghan (1912 – 2005) who said:

> *The Queen has a deep sense of duty and responsibility in [the political] area, and also sees it as a means of preserving the Royal Family as an institution. If her Prime Minister liked to give the Queen information and gossip about certain political characters, she would listen very attentively, for she has a real understanding of the value of a constitutional monarchy. I think she is absolutely right to be on the alert. I think the prestige of the monarchy could deteriorate if she didn't work so hard at it ... She really knows about preserving the monarchy and how to conduct herself on public occasions. When to step into the limelight and when to step out. She really is professional in her approach ...*

Callaghan said that a Prime Minister in dealing with the Queen gets friendliness, not friendship. This view was endorsed by the Foreign Secretary in his government, David

Owen (born 1938) who spoke about the Queen's ability to have an intelligent conversation on a subject without actually revealing what she personally thinks about it. He also noted that she did not seem at all bothered about her "image" when surrounded by a scrum of photographers and journalists.

PRINCESS ANNE GETS MARRIED

The first of the royal children to marry was Princess Anne. In the modern age, there were no arranged royal marriages but it is speculated that the Queen and Prince Philip were not terribly impressed by Anne's choice of husband.

Captain Mark Phillips, a professional soldier from a respectable middle-class background, was as obsessed as Anne was with horses, to the extent that her mother is rumored to have said, "I shouldn't wonder if their children are four-legged." Prince Charles, serving at the time with the Royal Navy in the Caribbean, told a friend that it was "such a ghastly mismatch." He famously gave his brother-in-law the nickname "Foggy," so dull did he find him.

One royal relative said of him, "If you ever sat next to Mark Phillips you had to know about army maneuvers or dressage, and if you didn't know about either of those subjects you'd had it." Anne usually got her way and despite all the misgivings of others, the couple were married at Westminster Abbey on November 14, 1973, which was also Charles's 25th birthday.

KIDNAP ATTEMPT

Princess Anne's popularity soared around this time as she emerged as a hard-working, straight-talking woman. This was even more the case following an attempt to kidnap her in March the following year when she and her new husband were returning to Buckingham Palace after attending a charity event.

On the Mall their car was stopped by another vehicle. The driver, Ian Ball, leapt out with a gun in his hand and opened fire. Anne's personal protection officer, Inspector James Beaton (born 1943), got out of the Princess's car and tried to shield her and to disarm Ball. Beaton's Walther PPK jammed and Ball shot him.

Anne's driver, Alex Callender, was also shot by Ball as he tried to disarm him. A tabloid journalist who had been nearby, Brian McConnell, was shot in the chest as he tried to intervene. Ball went up to Anne in the car and told her he was kidnapping her for ransom that he then intended to give to the NHS.

When he told her to get out of the car, she reportedly replied, "Not bloody likely!" She got out of the other side of the car with a lady-in-waiting who was with her. At that moment, a pedestrian, former boxer Ron Russell approached Ball from behind and punched him in the back of the head before leading the Princess away from the scene.

A police officer, Peter Edmonds, who chanced upon the incident was also shot by Ball but he had already called for back-up and Ball was arrested.

Fortunately all involved recovered from their wounds. Beaton was awarded the George Cross while Russell was awarded the George Medal and Callender, McConnell, and Edmonds were awarded the Queen's Medal for Gallantry. Having pleaded guilty to attempted murder and kidnapping, Ball was detained under the Mental Health Act.

Captain Mark Phillips

Mark Anthony Peter Phillips (born 1948) is the grandson of a brigadier who served as Aide-de-Camp to George VI from 1947 until 1950. In 1969, he was commissioned as a second lieutenant in the Queen's Dragoon Guards and was promoted to lieutenant in 1971. He was working as a Personal Aide-de-Camp to the Queen from 1974. Promotion to captain followed in 1975. He retired from the army in 1978 but continued to call himself Captain Mark Phillips.

Captain Phillips met Princess Anne at the Munich Olympics in 1972. A member of the British equestrian team, he won a three-day event gold medal, having already won a world championship and a European championship. He and Princess Anne were married in November 1973 and had two children, Peter (born 1977) and Zara (born 1981).

In 1985, he was named in a paternity suit as father of a child as a result of an affair with a New Zealand art teacher Heather Tonkin, and in 1992 he and Princess Anne were divorced. Five years later, in 1997, he married American Olympic dressage rider Sandy Pflueger (born 1954). Their daughter Stephanie was born in 1997. The couple separated in 2012.

Captain Phillips is now in a relationship with 38-year-old American Olympic show jumper Lauren Hough (born 1979). He remains a leading figure in British equestrian circles, a noted eventing course designer, and a columnist in *Horse & Hound* magazine.

Mounted bands of the Household Cavalry at Trooping the Color. The rider of the piebald (black-and-white) drum horse, working the reins with his feet, crosses drumsticks above his head in salute.

TROOPING THE COLOR

Held in London annually in Horseguards Parade, on a Saturday in June, Trooping the Color is a ceremony that has been a tradition of the British and Commonwealth armies since the seventeenth century, although its origins are thought to go back even further than that.

A regiment's colors, or flags, represent its ethos as well as its fallen soldiers and in the past acted as a rallying point on the battlefield. In the ceremony, one of the foot-guard regiment's colors are paraded through the ranks of guards followed by a march-past of the entire Household Division.

Since 1748, the ceremony has also marked the official birthday of the sovereign in June when it is felt that there is a better chance of fine weather, permitting the parade and celebrations to be staged outside. The Queen's real birthday is, of course, April 21st.

THE SILVER JUBILEE 1977

At first glance, it did not seem like the best moment to celebrate the Queen's twenty-five years on the throne. Britain was experiencing the worst economic period since the war. Inflation was soaring out of control to 16 percent and the unemployment figures made grim reading. Public expenditure was slashed after a huge loan had to be solicited from the International Monetary Fund. No one was much in the mood for a party.

It was a busy year for the Queen, however, and she traveled 56,000 miles visiting the nations of the Commonwealth. In February, she was in American Samoa, Western Samoa, Tonga, Fiji, and New Zealand where she carried out the State Opening of Parliament. In March, she crossed the Tasman Sea to Australia where she performed the same duty in Canberra. Toward the end of the month she could be found in Papua New Guinea and then, on the way home, Muscat.

But with the Government having very little to spend on the celebration in June, Her Majesty might have been justified in feeling a little apprehensive as the Jubilee approached. She may also have been apprehensive about the fact that her Jubilee tour included Northern Ireland. But she insisted that the visit to Ulster would go ahead.

GOD SAVE THE QUEEN

Punk Rock might also have given Her Majesty cause for concern, if such a musical genre appeared on the royal radar. As the Jubilee approached, punk was at its peak. The leading punk rock band The Sex Pistols were storming the charts and in danger of occupying the top spot on Jubilee day itself. Their anarchic single *God Save the Queen* included the lyrics "God save the queen/She's not a human being/and There's no future/In England's dreaming."

Jubilee day arrived, however, and there was nothing to worry about. The nation was collectively relieved to have something to celebrate at last. Everyone partied and showed their continued affection for the monarch.

Flags were flown, street parties were enjoyed, and bonfires were lit. It seemed that people wanted to send a message of appreciation for all that the Queen had done for the country, for her devotion to duty, her honor, and her general decency. Her domestic chaplain said:

She was floored. She could not believe that people had that much affection for her as a person and she was embarrassed and at the same time terribly touched by it all.

A FADING LOVE AFFAIR

In some Commonwealth countries, however, there was a feeling that the love affair with the British monarchy was fading. Elizabeth went to Canada in 1978 as part of her tour but also to open the Commonwealth Games being held in Edmonton, Alberta. She had visited the country perhaps a dozen times during her reign and perhaps they were becoming too familiar with her.

There was also a bad feeling about the relationship with Britain on the part of French Canadians. On this visit, the French Canadian Prime Minister of Canada, the charismatic Pierre Trudeau (1919 – 2000), failed to turn up to welcome her to the country. He did not want to be seen by his fellow French-Canadians to be endorsing the Queen's position as Canadian head of state.

CHAPTER 18

DIANA AND THE DEPUTY QUEEN

LADY DIANA SPENCER

The marriage of the heir to the throne was vitally important to the survival of the British monarchy. Unfortunately Prince Charles was in love with a married woman, Camilla Parker-Bowles (born 1947). The couple's relationship was not entirely unknown in their circle. They had met in 1971, but the relationship ended in early 1973 when he joined the Royal Navy.

It was suggested that Lord Mountbatten brought it to an end by arranging for Charles to be posted overseas. Ultimately, Mounbatten had wanted Charles to marry his granddaughter, Amanda Knatchbull (born 1957). Charles is reported to have proposed to her, but following the assassination of Mountbatten and other members of her family, she was reluctant to become a royal and declined.

Charles turned again to Mrs. Parker-Bowles. Like his great-uncle Edward VIII before him, he was caught between his duty as a member of the royal family and his love for a woman. But Charles was under pressure to get married and his bride had to have a pristine history. Lady Diana Spencer (1961 – 97) seemed to be the ideal solution.

The two met for the first time in November 1977. Charles had been dating Diana's older sister, Lady Sarah Spencer, but transferred his attentions to Diana in the summer of 1980. By this time Diana was 19 and the courtship blossomed. She was invited to Balmoral where his family took a liking to her. Charles proposed to Diana on February 6, 1981, and the engagement became official on February 24. The couple were married at St. Paul's Cathedral on July 29, 1981, and became the Prince and Princess of Wales.

ENTER THE DEPUTY QUEEN

Change was again in the air in Britain. The bitter strikes of the Winter of Discontent of 1978 to 1979 and economic instability led to the downfall of the Callaghan government. A year after their defeat in the 1974 general election, the Conservative Party had elected Margaret Thatcher (1925 – 2013) as their leader to replace Edward Heath. She won the 1979 general election with a majority of 43 seats and became Britain's and Europe's first elected female head of state.

It was a significant change for the Queen, having to deal with her first woman prime minister who was, in fact, just six months older than her. The relationship immediately caught the interest of the press and the media.

Mrs. Thatcher was dubbed the "Deputy Queen" due to her self-assuredness and frequent arrogance. They had much in common, both professional women devoted to their jobs, both with supportive husbands and both determined to maintain their nation's position in the world.

AN EXAGGERATED RESPECT

But there were a great many differences too. The Queen was conservative and averse to change while Margaret Thatcher was revolutionary and determined to change Britain for good. Although their husbands got on very well, the two women were uncomfortable in each other's company.

THE ROYAL WEDDING

The "Wedding of the Century" took place on July 29, 1981, at St. Paul's Cathedral, London, when Lady Diana Spencer married Charles, Prince of Wales, and became Diana, Princess of Wales. The ceremony was a traditional Church of England wedding service. Notable figures in attendance included many members of royal families from across the world, republican heads of state, and members of the bride's and groom's families.

Their marriage was widely billed as a "fairytale wedding," and was watched by an estimated global TV audience of 750 million. The United Kingdom had a national holiday on that day to mark the wedding. The couple separated in 1992 and divorced in 1996. The fairy tale was well and truly destroyed when later reports emerged that their relationship was deeply flawed and the marriage may have been doomed from the start.

Diana, Princess of Wales, is often informally referred to as "Princess Diana," although this is not a title she ever officially held. Newspapers and television sometimes even refer to her as "Lady Di," which recollects her days as Lady Diana Spencer. In a speech after her death, Prime Minister Tony Blair called Diana "The People's Princess," a title which resonated with the British population at the time, and has remained with her ever since.

THE PEOPLE'S PRINCESS

Diana, Princess of Wales (Diana Frances; née Spencer; 1961 – 97), was the first wife of Charles, Prince of Wales, who is the eldest child and heir apparent of Queen Elizabeth II. The Spencer family were undeniably aristocratic with links to the great families of England and could even claim royal blood that could be traced back to the first Duke of Richmond (1519 – 36), illegitimate son of Henry VIII (1491 – 1547). The family was wealthy, with a stately home, Althorp, in Northamptonshire. Their London property, Spencer House was home to expensive collections of paintings, furniture, and art. The family had traditionally been courtiers and even on Diana's mother's side there were royal connections, living as they did next door to Sandringham. Diana's father, the 8th Earl Spencer (1924 – 92) had been equerry to George VI as well as to Queen Elizabeth.

FAIRY TALE PRINCESS

Lady Diana's parents divorced when she was 7 years old and she was firstly educated at home before attending various private schools. She was not academic, however, failing her O-Levels twice. After finishing school in Switzerland, she embarked on a series of low-paid jobs. When she became engaged to Prince Charles, she was working at a nursery in London and was thirteen years younger than him. On July 29, 1981, she and the Prince were married at St. Paul's Cathedral in a wedding that was consistently described as "fairy tale," a term that would come back to haunt the couple. A global television audience of 750 million tuned in and 600,000 people lined the streets of London.

The couple lived at Kensington Palace and Highgrove House in Gloucestershire and very soon their first child, Prince William (born 1982) was born, followed by Prince Harry in 1984. She treated her children in an entirely different way to other children of the royal family, taking William with her and her husband, for instance, on a tour of Australia and New Zealand. She retained control of all aspects of her children, choosing their Christian names, their schools and clothing. She personally took them to school as often as possible.

IRRETRIEVABLE BREAKDOWN

Amid sensational press speculation, Charles and Diana's marriage collapsed, their age difference being one factor and Charles's ongoing affair with Camilla Parker-Bowles being another. The Princess had a five-year affair with Major James Hewitt (born 1958) and the 1992 book *Diana: Her True Story* by Andrew Morton (born 1953) revealed her unhappiness, creating a whirlwind of press attention. A further affair with James Gilbey created a scandal known as Squidgygate from Gilbey's affectionate name for Diana learned from tapes that were released of their private conversations.

More tapes—this time featuring intimate conversations between Prince Charles and Camilla Parker-Bowles—emerged in November 1992. The following month the Prime Minister announced in the Commons that Charles and Diana had separated. In a televised interview in June 1994, Prince Charles confirmed that he had been having an affair since 1986, but that it had begun only after his marriage to Princess Diana had "irretrievably broken down."

THE QUEEN OF PEOPLE'S HEARTS

In November 1995 Diana gave an interview on *Panorama* in which she admitted to having been in love with James Hewitt. She also confessed to having suffered from depression, "rampant bulimia" and that she had self-harmed on a number of occasions during her marriage. In a reference to Camilla Parker-Bowles, she famously said: "Well, there were three of us in this marriage, so it was a bit crowded." She told her interviewer "I'd like to be a queen of people's hearts." In July 1996 the Prince and Princess of Wales were divorced. At Charles's insistence, Diana lost the right to be called "Her Royal Highness" and was to be called "Diana, Princess of Wales."

Diana became celebrated for her charity work after her divorce as well as for her work in support of the International Campaign to Ban Landmines. But she remained the target of the world's media. She died in a car crash in Paris on August 31, 1997, while being pursued by paparazzi. Her companion Dodi Fayed (1955 – 97) and their chauffeur, Henri Paul (1956 – 97), also died in the crash. Diana's death was followed by a near mass hysterical reaction in Britain. Her funeral brought a viewing audience in Britain alone of 32 million while millions more watched around the world.

Mrs. Thatcher had no sense of humor and the Queen rather liked people who were witty and entertaining. Perhaps Mrs. Thatcher's attitude toward the monarchy might be explained in a friend's comment:

She had a rather exaggerated respect for the institution of monarchy. Nobody would curtsy lower—no one would be more supportive of the monarchy even when it was engaged in attacking her.

CONFERENCE IN A WAR ZONE

There were many things about Mrs. Thatcher's government which made the Queen unhappy, by all accounts. One of the principal points of disagreement was over the Commonwealth and especially southern Africa where the Queen did not support the segregation policies of the governments of South Africa and Rhodesia. Sanctions were in place against Rhodesia following its unilateral declaration of independence and Margaret Thatcher was not totally in favor of either the sanctions or black initiatives for equality in the region.

These issues were to be discussed at the Commonwealth Conference to be held in Lusaka in Zambia. Thatcher, however, said that she would not be able to get another year of sanctions against Rhodesia through the House of Commons, thus derailing preparations for the conference. The situation deteriorated further when Rhodesia bombed Lusaka.

The New Zealand Prime Minister Robert Muldoon (1921 – 92), playing to a right-wing audience at home, advised the Queen not to go to the conference as it was taking place in what he called a "war zone."

Elizabeth had only ever missed one biennial Commonwealth heads of Government meeting and was determined to attend. In the end, the nationalist leader Joshua Nkomo (1917 – 99) was persuaded to call a cease-fire while she was there.

THE QUEEN AS PEACEMAKER

Mrs. Thatcher's Foreign Secretary at the time, Lord Carrington (born 1919) said the conference had "all the hallmarks of being very unpleasant, and not to say a disaster." The Queen, he added, "played an enormous role in calming everything down." On his boss Mrs. Thatcher, Carrington was crystal clear:

Thatcher was viewed with a great deal of suspicion by all the Africans, and most of the Asians, and in fact by most of the Commonwealth.

However, thanks to the Queen acting as peacemaker, the improved atmosphere at the conference led to an agreement on the future of Rhodesia which would become the independent state of Zimbabwe. But Mrs. Thatcher continued to irritate Her Majesty on matters involving her beloved Commonwealth.

Six months after the Thatcher government came to power, in order to economize, the Ministry of Education announced, without any consultation, the introduction of higher student fees for overseas students. Until then, Commonwealth students could come to Britain and pay the same fees as British students. The Queen made no secret of her concern.

CONFRONTATIONAL AND DIVISIVE

Mrs. Thatcher's relationship with the Commonwealth remained fractious. She believed that the imposition of sanctions on South Africa was harming British exports and she argued, too, that it was not good for black South Africans who would lose their jobs as a result. Sanctions, however, were generally viewed in the Commonwealth as a means of getting rid of apartheid.

Mrs. Thatcher argued at several conferences with other leaders, issued her own statements that sometimes seemed to the others to contradict what had actually been agreed.

A crisis in the relationship between the two women arose when the *Sunday Times* published an article claiming that:

> *Sources close to the Queen let it be known to the Sunday Times that she is dismayed by many of Mrs. Thatcher's policies This dismay goes well beyond the current crisis in the Commonwealth over South Africa. In an unprecedented disclosure of the monarch's views, it was said that the Queen considers the Prime Minister's approach to be uncaring, confrontational and divisive.*

BAD FEELING AT THE PALACE

It was indeed unprecedented, and the Queen must have been horrified at such a disclosure. For her part, Margaret Thatcher must have been very hurt and it is interesting that the incident is not mentioned in her memoirs. Doubt was expressed as to whether the leak was, firstly true, and secondly whether it had actually emanated from the Palace.

Sir William Heseltine wrote to the *Times* about it, saying that "Whatever personal opinions the sovereign may hold or may have expressed to the Government, she is bound to accept and act on the advice of her Government." He also wrote that what is said between the Queen and her Prime Minister is strictly confidential. He finished by insisting that the newspaper claiming that the details of the article came from Palace sources "constitutes a totally unjustified slur on the impartiality and discretion of senior members of the Royal Household."

Caught in the middle of all this was the Queen's new Press Secretary, Michael Shea (1938 – 2009). It was he who had given the interview to the *Sunday Times* journalist, Simon Freeman, who Shea felt had betrayed him by taking his words and twisting them into what appeared in the newspaper. Nonetheless, there certainly was a bad feeling toward Margaret Thatcher at Buckingham Palace.

CANADA IS SETTLED

The Queen's diplomatic skills were put to the test when Canadian Prime Minister Pierre Trudeau proposed constitutional changes in Canada that would bring an end to the British government's constitutional role in the country. The Queen found herself caught between the republican French-speaking minority based in Quebec, and the more conservative majority who were in favor of the monarchy.

Behind the scenes the Queen became involved in negotiating the terms of the legislation to bring about a change to the British role in Canada. Finally in January 1982, the British government passed the Canada Act. This brought to an end British executive authority in Canada but the monarchy was preserved.

The functions of the monarch were transferred to the governor-general, but the Queen retained her position as Queen of Canada and her role was all the more palatable to Canadians because she was no longer identified with the country's constitutional issues.

TASK FORCE TO THE SOUTH ATLANTIC

When Mrs. Thatcher went to war with Argentina over the invasion of the Falkland Islands in the South Atlantic, the Queen was closely consulted. As sovereign of a country whose sovereignty is under attack by another nation she was deeply involved, especially as her government had decided to recapture the islands.

Although the Queen was head of the Commonwealth, of which the Falklands were part, and was head of Britain's armed forces, however, she was also concerned on another entirely personal level. Her son, Prince Andrew, was a naval helicopter pilot and he insisted on going to the Falklands. A decision which made the Queen extremely proud.

Sub Lieutenant Prince Andrew embarked on his first front line tour of duty on April 5, 1982, onboard the aircraft carrier HMS *Invincible*.

Margaret Thatcher

Margaret Hilda Thatcher, Baroness Thatcher (1925 – 2013) was an extraordinary figure who changed Britain and British politics forever. Born Margaret Roberts, the daughter of a grocer in the Lincolnshire town of Grantham, her father was also an Alderman and sat on the municipal council of the town.

She won a place to study chemistry at Somerville College, Oxford, graduating in 1947. In 1949, at age just 23, she was selected by the Conservative Party to contest Dartford with little chance of winning. She also stood there in the 1950 and 1951 elections. She married Dennis Thatcher in December 1951 and gave birth to twins, Carol and Mark, in 1953. She studied law and became a barrister in 1954, at Lincoln's Inn, one of the four Inns of Court in London.

HIGH-PITCHED AND IRRITATING

In 1958, she was selected for the safe Conservative seat of Finchley which she represented until her retirement in 1992. In 1961 she was appointed a junior pensions minister and in 1967, with Harold Wilson's Labour in power, she was promoted to the shadow cabinet by party leader Edward Heath. Following the Conservative victory of 1970, she became education secretary and was the only woman in the Cabinet. When she ended universal free school milk for children, she became known as "Thatcher the milk-snatcher."

Then in the middle of power cuts and a three-day working week in February 1974, Edward Heath called a general election and lost. In 1975, Mrs. Thatcher defeated Heath for the leadership of the Conservative Party and went on to become Britain's first woman prime minister when the Conservatives won the 1979 general election. Her victory was against all the odds and she was attacked in the press for her clothes, her hair, and especially her voice which at the time was high-pitched and irritating.

GETTING POLITICALLY SERIOUS

Her advisors began work on her however. They softened her appearance and her hair style, and upgraded her wardrobe. Then a vocal coach taught her how to lower her voice when making speeches and public appearances. Her tones became deeper and more resonant, and as a result she sounded more like a serious politician.

She championed monetarism in fiscal management to begin with. In her first budget VAT was increased to 15 percent, almost double what it had been. Personal income tax was cut and the top rate of income tax was lowered from 83 percent to 60 percent. In the years that followed, she continued to cut taxes and unemployment rose to 3 million.

She will always be remembered for her defeat of the trade unions whose actions had brought down the Callaghan government. Employment acts brought in secret ballots when trade unions sought strike action and in the late 1980s the closed shop and secondary strike actions were made illegal.

THE IRON LADY

On October 12, 1984, the IRA almost killed Mrs. Thatcher when they blew up the Grand Hotel in Brighton where she was staying during the Conservative Party conference. It did not stop her from delivering her speech later that same day.

She is most closely identified with the Falklands War and it could be said to have rescued her premiership. When Argentina invaded the Falkland Islands in April 1982, Thatcher ignored the advice of her Cabinet and assembled a task force to recapture the islands. The Argentineans surrendered and a year later she was returned to power with a large majority.

During her thirteen years in office, Mrs. Thatcher's unrelenting anti-Communism and uncompromising leadership earned her the nickname "Iron Lady" in the Russian press and she became a leading force in undermining the Soviet Union. She was re-elected for a third term in 1987, but during this period she became widely unpopular across the country. She resigned as prime minister and party leader in November 1990 and retired to the House of Lords in 1992.

Always controversial, Margaret Thatcher is seen as one of the greatest politicians in British history. Her legacy of social and economic policies, known as Thatcherism, went on to influence subsequent British governments for the next twenty-five years. She died on April 8, 2013, after a stroke, at age 87.

Margaret Thatcher was prime minister of the United Kingdom from 1979 to 1990. She was the longest-serving prime minister of the twentieth century, and the first woman to hold the office.

The Prince set sail as part of the Task Force sent to the South Atlantic to regain the Falkland Islands. Throughout the conflict he saw active service flying on multiple missions including anti-surface warfare, Exocet missile decoy, and casualty evacuation. HMS *Invincible* returned to Portsmouth Naval Base on September 17, 1982, and was met by the Queen and the Duke of Edinburgh.

THE QUEEN'S ISLANDS

That same year saw fighting in another part of the Commonwealth. On the Caribbean island of Grenada, where Elizabeth is head of state, the Prime Minister had been killed in a left-wing coup. The Governor-General, Sir Paul Scoon (1935 – 2013) asked the United States President Ronald Reagan (1911 – 2004) for help. American troops were sent and quickly restored order.

Neither the Queen nor the Prime Minister were told about the invasion by the Americans. Mrs. Thatcher was especially surprised at the act because of her close relationship with Ronald Reagan, and told the President that he should have asked for the consent of the Queen and her Prime Minister. Later she recalled exclaiming to Reagan: "They're the Queen's islands!"

FAMILIES WERE DIVIDED

The Miners' Strike of 1984 to 1985 was a horrendous time for Britain. Mrs. Thatcher had decided to take on the National Union of Mineworkers and the result was months of pitched battles between pickets and police.

The coal mines were shut down for a year in a bitter strike that saw miners physically fighting with the police in many places. The result was mass closures of the coal mines and privatization of the coal industry.

Indeed, privatization was one of the central planks of the Thatcher philosophy and many industries were sold off—Ferranti, Cable and Wireless, North Sea Oil, British Ports, British Telecom, British Gas, British Airways, and water and electricity followed suit.

Families were divided and people suffered. The Queen must inevitably have been upset by the strike, especially when she read letters from miners' families describing the dire situation in which they found themselves.

A jubilant Prince Andrew is met by his proud father Prince Philip, after the aircraft carrier HMS *Invincible* sailed home from the Falklands to a tumultuous welcome at Portsmouth on September 17, 1982.

MODERNIZING THE ROYAL HOUSEHOLD

During the 1980s there was renewed debate about the finances of the royal household. *Fortune* magazine, still paying no heed to claims that the royal palaces and collections could not be included in estimates of the Queen's wealth, gauged her to be worth £7 billion and that her fortune was going up by about £3 million a day. Such news was seized on by the British tabloid newspapers.

Around this time, Her Majesty ordered a reappraisal of the structure of the Royal Household. It was undertaken by Lord Airlie (born 1926) who had been appointed Lord Chamberlain (head of the household) in 1984. Airlie, who was an experienced businessman and had known the Queen for his entire life, brought in Peat Marwick McLintock who were already the Queen's auditors to carry out a review.

The Palace had lost control in recent decades over functions such as the maintenance of palaces and royal transport and it wanted to re-establish some independence once more. The result of the report was the modernization of the royal household. A proper personnel department was created and offices and budgeting systems were introduced.

In such a conservative institution these changes did not prove popular but they were essential, especially as they enabled the Palace to gain more independence. It took control of the Civil List from the Treasury, for example. The Civil List was increased that year by 50 percent and would amount to £7.9 million a year during the next ten years, beginning at the start of 1991.

The Department of the Environment also handed management of royal property back to the royal household. They even succeeded in cutting costs, from the £21 million spent by the Government down to £17 million.

Meanwhile, the Conservative Party had had enough of Margaret Thatcher and after eleven years as Prime Minister she was forced out of office. She was replaced by John Major (born 1946) in November 1990, the ninth prime minister of Elizabeth II's reign.

AN INTRUDER AT THE PALACE

At 7:15 a.m. on July 9, 1982, the Queen was wakened by the sound of her bedroom door opening followed by footsteps across the floor. It was dark and she knew that it could not be her footman who was out walking the dogs. She said in as officious a voice as possible: "It's too early yet for tea." Perhaps, she thought one of the Palace staff had opened the wrong door in error. The voice of the Queen was sure to stop them in their tracks.

But the person who had entered the room was unperturbed by the unmistakable sound of the Queen's voice. Instead he walked over to the curtains and opened them. Incredibly, the intruder was a 33-year-old unemployed house painter who suffered from schizophrenia. Father of four, Michael Fagan had scaled the Palace's 14-foot wall, negotiated the barbed wire and spikes on the top, and then climbed a drainpipe before wandering into the monarch's bedroom.

An alarm had gone off, but thinking it faulty, the police officers guarding the building switched it off. Fagan had broken a glass ashtray in another room and when he entered the bedroom, he was carrying a shard of glass. It was initially reported that he had sat on her bed, but the Queen later said that she had left her bedroom immediately to get help.

She had already twice telephoned the Palace switchboard to summon help but none arrived. Eventually her footman arrived with two police officers and Fagan was arrested. He was committed for psychiatric evaluation and after spending six months in a psychiatric hospital, was released.

His mother said of the incident: "He thinks so much of the Queen. I can imagine him just wanting to simply talk and say hello and discuss his problems."

Apparently, during the entire incident, the Queen remained calm and immediately afterward returned to bed to drink a cup of tea. Fagan later said he had intended to slash his wrists in front of her.

CHAPTER 19

AT WAR WITH THE QUEEN OF HEARTS

The year 1992 was very bad for the Queen and the royal family. The pressure on them regarding finances mounted, especially after it was revealed that the royals paid no tax.

This was coupled with the perception of the younger royals leading privileged existences while the British people suffered as the economy stumbled. The exemption on royal tax had been introduced for George VI and continued with his daughter. In 1991, the Queen asked her advisors to open discussions with the Treasury on the matter.

"ANNUS HORRIBILIS"

As if things were not bad enough, on the night of November 20, 1992, a major fire broke out at Windsor Castle, causing significant and widespread damage to the Upper Ward. It was believed to have been caused by a spotlight setting a curtain alight while repair work was being done in a private chapel.

Apart from fire and smoke damage there was considerable damage caused by the vast amount of water used to fight the flames. Immediately after, there was a vigorous political debate about where the funds were going to come from to make the necessary extensive repairs.

The castle was owned by the Crown and was, therefore, maintained by the government. It was not insured in an effort to save money. In the press it was argued that the Queen should pay for the repairs herself. Ultimately, it was decided to pay for the repairs by opening Buckingham Palace to the public several times a year and by charging the public to use the parkland that surrounded Windsor Castle.

Four days after the fire, Elizabeth, stricken with a bad cold and the after-effects of the smoke and fumes, gave a speech at a luncheon at Guildhall in the City of London to celebrate the fortieth year of her reign. The speech attempted to gain the support of the public, hinting at changes to come but it also included

Windsor Castle on fire in November 1992.

bitter references to the press. These were not overt in nature but demonstrated yet again that those around her still did not recognize the importance of the media in reflecting the feelings of the British people.

She did allude to her decision to pay tax but may have elicited more sympathy had this been announced properly in advance of the speech. Elizabeth famously expressed her feelings about the year that she and her family had experienced:

> 1992 is not a year on which I shall look back with undiluted pleasure. In the words of one of my more sympathetic correspondents, it has turned out to be an "Annus Horribilis."

KNEEJERK REACTION

With Windsor Castle still smoldering, Prime Minister John Major made an unexpected announcement in the House of Commons. He told MPs that the Queen and Prince Charles had agreed to pay income tax and that five members of the royal family—Princess Margaret, the Princess Royal as Princess Anne was now titled, the Duke of York, Prince Edward, and Princess Alice the Duchess of Gloucester (1901–2004)—would from now on be paid from the Duchy of Lancaster.

It was a response to the tide of public opinion in favor of such a move. Unfortunately, it appeared to be simply a kneejerk reaction to criticism of the the royal family. It was a public relations disaster.

During that terrible year there was more bad news on the horizon, however, concerning Prince Charles's marriage.

A COUPLE AT WAR

What was really threatening the image of the royal family, however, was the collapse of the marriage of Charles and Diana. On December 9, the announcement was made that the couple were to separate. The Prime Minister said that "the decision had been reached amicably" and that the couple would continue with their public duties and would "from time to time attend family occasions and national events together."

The wish was expressed on behalf of the Queen and her husband that "the intrusions into the privacy of the Prince and Princess may now cease." He went on to confirm the position regarding the constitution:

> ... the decision to separate has no constitutional implications. The Succession to the Throne is unaffected by it; the children of the Prince and Princess retain their position in the line of succession; and there is no reason why the Princess of Wales should not be crowned Queen in due course. The Prince of Wales's succession as head of the Church of England is also unaffected.

Of course, the idea that Diana, in such circumstances, could be Charles's consort seemed ridiculous and his position regarding the Church of England seemed fairly hypocritical, but it was supported by the Archbishop of Canterbury who said that:

> a formal separation within marriage would be likely to win widespread understanding, as it would signal the importance of the institution of marriage and the seriousness of the marriage vows made before God.

CAMILLAGATE

Then the "Camillagate" scandal happened, featuring another in the series of leaked tapes collected from hacked telephone calls. The public were now able to listen in on Charles and Mrs. Parker-Bowles talking in highly intimate terms.

There was little doubt left that Diana's fears about Charles and Camilla's relationship were grounded in reality. There were even suggestions that the graphic nature of the Camillagate conversation could stop Charles ever becoming King.

The "War of the Waleses" was devastating to the Queen and to the public perception of the monarchy that she had spent her life carefully preserving. The warring couple used the media to damage each other and Diana was now becoming a serious threat to the royal family. No one quite knew what she would do next.

Diana was a beautiful and glamorous woman, and her charity work was widely respected. Meanwhile, the royal family looked increasingly stuffy and were getting more and more perturbed by her behavior. A courtier summed up the attitude of the court toward her, "They're all terrified of her at the Palace," he said.

PRINCESS IN LOVE

In December 1993, Princess Diana sensationally announced that she was withdrawing from public life. She made sure to thank the Queen and Prince Philip for their "support and understanding," but pointedly made no reference to Prince Charles. This had the effect of suggesting that perhaps he and his people had forced this withdrawal.

While Diana was creating the press headlines, Princess Anne was quietly getting married for a second time, to Commander Tim Laurence (born 1955) the Queen's Equerry. The marriage was a surprise to the royal family. The Queen reportedly only heard of it from the BBC. The wedding took place at Crathie Church near Balmoral Castle, as the Church of Scotland allowed divorcees to marry in church.

But the press coverage of Princess Diana continued unabated and a 1994 book, *Princess in Love* by Anna Pasternak, revealed her relationship with James Hewitt. Then the *News of the World* published a story about another of Diana's lovers, art dealer Oliver Hoare.

After the affair ended, Hoare, a friend of Prince Charles, received a number of nuisance phone calls from Diana. Next, she was photographed sunbathing topless in Spain but the pictures were bought by the owner of *Hello* magazine to stop them being published.

THE FIGHTBACK BEGINS

Throughout all of this, the Queen is reported to have been very low, confessing as such to guests at private dinner parties. Members of the royal family were quarreling among themselves. The tabloid newspapers were relentless in their pursuit of gossip and scandal and photos of Diana. When the Queen invited her to Sandringham for Christmas in 1993, the paparazzi were interested only in Diana and, to

Elizabeth's chagrin, virtually ignored the rest of the family.

Prince Charles had inevitably gone down in the public's estimation and he was determined to revive his image. Television was the medium he chose and Jonathan Dimbleby was the interviewer he wanted. The program—*Charles, The Private Man, The Public* Role—was dressed up as a celebration of the twenty-fifth anniversary of Charles's investiture as Prince of Wales and featured an interview and film of his charity work and his role. It aired on ITV on June 29, 1994.

The Queen had no involvement and, indeed, along with friends and courtiers, thought it was a bad idea. As ever, her inclination would have been to remain silent and wait for time to pass and the noise to die down. Even Camilla Parker-Bowles pleaded with Charles not to go through with it. For the Prince, however, it was an attempt to bring a halt to the endless speculation.

Princess Diana with Prince William (right) and Prince Harry at Thorpe Park Resort in April 1993.

THE CRUX OF THE MATTER

Dimbleby's question "Did you try to be faithful?" and Charles's answer that he did, until the marriage had "irretrievably broken down," was the crux of the matter. Ultimately, Charles did well and there was a positive response from the public to his candor.

Dimbleby followed up the interview with a biography of Prince Charles, but the Queen was furious when she learned that the presenter had been allowed access to state papers during his research. Her anger at her son was evident from the fact that on the annual pilgrimage to the Highlands, Charles stayed with the Queen Mother at Birkhall.

The book was serialized in the *Sunday Times* as the Queen embarked on a historic visit to Russia, the first time a British monarch had visited the country and instead of her trip, the newspapers were full of the revelations in the book. Her parenting skills were questioned, as was the distance of the Queen from her children, and Philip's bullying of Charles.

Diana turned out to be a neurotic woman after he married her, it claimed. But Mrs. Parker-Bowles emerged with flying colors as the one genuinely nice person in Charles's circle. The British public did not agree, however, and she was reportedly spat upon while out shopping. In the middle of all this, Camilla and her husband separated, having been married for twenty years.

THE QUEEN OF HEARTS

A year later, on November 20, 1995, Diana gave an interview to journalist Martin Bashir (born 1963) on the BBC current affairs program *Panorama*, watched by a staggering 23 million viewers. No one knew anything about it, not even Lord Hussey (1923 – 2006), chairman of the BBC Board of Governors whose wife, Lady Susan Hussey (born 1939) was a Lady-in-Waiting to the Queen.

Like Charles, Diana was in the mood to confess, talking about her bulimia, her depression, and the third person in their marriage. She admitted that she had an affair with James Hewitt but denied that she had had other affairs. She said that she did not want a divorce and told Bashir that she wanted to be "a queen of people's hearts." She also raised doubts as to Charles's suitability for the throne:

> *Because I know the character I would think that the top job, as I call it, would bring enormous limitations to him, and I don't know whether he could adapt to that.*

TERMS AND CONDITIONS

The Queen was undoubtedly horrified and despairing of the damage that was being caused to the monarchy for which she had worked so hard all her life. Deciding it was time for action, she wrote to the warring couple that they should launch divorce proceedings. It was no secret, and the Palace issued a statement that she had done so.

The discussions about the divorce were supposed to remain confidential, but the Palace was furious to learn that Diana had issued details to the newspapers. She revealed she had agreed to Charles's request for a divorce so long as she would be involved in decisions regarding the Princes William and Harry; that she would continue to live at Kensington Palace; and that she would no longer be known as Her Royal Highness, but would be styled Diana, Princess of Wales.

A dispute arose between the two parties over the "HRH" title, the Palace denying that the Queen or the Prince had asked her to renounce it. The issue remained unresolved. By July however, they had finally reached an agreement. Diana was to receive £15 million. She would remain a member of the royal family but would give up her royal title. She was permitted use of St. James's Palace and would be free to wear items of royal jewelry.

The marriage was dissolved on August 28, 1996. Diana was beloved by the public, however, and was generally believed to have been treated badly by a vindictive royal family.

But Diana might have considered herself lucky, however, compared to the Duchess of York. Her marriage to Prince Andrew had ended in divorce in May of the same year, but she was treated entirely differently by the Palace. Things were not helped by the Duchess's extravagance and constant exposure of details of her private life in the press. The media in the end turned her into a figure of derision.

THE PARIS CAR CRASH

As Charles's romance with Camilla Parker-Bowles became increasingly public, Princess Diana too made no effort to conceal her love life. By 1997 she was in a relationship with Dodi Fayed (1955 – 97), the son of Egyptian billionaire Mohamed Al-Fayed (born 1929), the controversial former owner of Harrods Department Store in London. In the early hours of Sunday, August 31, 1997, Diana and Dodi, with a bodyguard, Trevor Rees-Jones (born 1968), left the Ritz Hotel in Paris, owned by Dodi's father, in a Mercedes driven by the Ritz's head of security, Henri Paul.

A posse of paparazzi set off in pursuit of them and their vehicle. Traveling at speed, they crashed into a concrete pillar in a tunnel at the Pont d'Alma. Dodi and the driver were killed. At first it was thought that the Princess had survived the crash, but at 4:00 a.m., it was announced that she was dead. Trevor Rees-Jones was the only survivor. None of the occupants of the Mercedes had been wearing seat belts.

THE PEOPLE'S PRINCESS

The week that followed was extraordinary, even by the standards of the royal family. The grief for the dead Princess reached almost mass hysteria proportions and outright hostility was expressed toward the Queen firstly for the treatment of Diana and then because of her

Princess Diana is captured on the Ritz Hotel's security camera at 21:50 on August 30, 1997, a few hours before she died.

reaction to her death. Ever conservative in her approach to matters of importance, the Queen seemed to have decided to carry on with everyday matters. The family was in Balmoral and it was decided to stay there until the following Saturday, the day of Diana's funeral.

One matter of particular contention concerned the flag that flew above Buckingham Palace. Traditionally, the flagpole was unoccupied when the monarch was absent from the Palace. The world was aghast at the two decisions—to remain at Balmoral and not to fly a flag at half-mast above the Palace. It seemed uncaring and aloof. Tony Blair (born 1953), who had only recently been elected Prime Minister got it right when he described the Princess on the day of her death as "the People's Princess."

SPEAK TO US MA'AM

Around the same time, the royal family made the first of a number of mistakes. They attended church at Crathie and during the service there was no mention of the Princess's death. It was deliberate in order not to upset William and Harry, but it yet again gave the appearance of an uncaring family.

Then there was the matter of bringing Diana's body home and Prince Charles flew to Paris after the morning service at Crathie with the Princess's two sisters to bring the casket back to RAF Northolt. That evening Diana's brother, Earl Spencer (born 1964) said that he wanted his sister to have a royal funeral but the Palace was in a state of confusion, having no precedent for the funeral of a mother of the heir to the throne who was herself a non-royal. A committee was formed, headed by Lord Airlie and the funeral was set for the following Saturday, September 6, 1997.

As the week went on, hostility to the royal family increased, the Queen being described as "remote" and "insensitive." The *Daily Mirror* shouted on its front page "Speak to us Ma'am. Show us you care."

LESSONS TO BE LEARNED

The public mood began to win the day and the Queen's plans for a quiet funeral for Diana were shelved in favor of a state funeral. A union flag appeared at half-mast on the Palace flagpole on the morning of the funeral, the Queen and the Duke of Edinburgh having finally left Balmoral

Prince Philip, Prince William, Earl Spencer, Prince Harry, and Prince Charles walking behind the coffin at Princess Diana's funeral. Prince William recently revealed that it was one of the hardest things he has ever done.

for London on Friday. Charles had brought the young princes back on Thursday.

When the Queen arrived back at the Palace, she walked among the forests of floral tributes that had been left at the gates. She saw for herself the extent to which her people were affected by the death of Diana and possibly even sensed some of the ill-will that was being directed toward her.

In an attempt to calm matters, she appeared on television that evening, paying tribute to Diana, "an exceptional and gifted human being." She seemed to acknowledge, possibly for the first time ever, that something had been badly handled with the words:

> *I for one, believe there are lessons to be drawn from her life and from the extraordinary and moving reaction to her death.*

YOUR BLOOD FAMILY

An extraordinary week culminated in an extraordinary day—the day of Princess Diana's funeral. The service at Westminster Abbey is remembered especially for Elton John's re-worked version of his hit *Candle in the Wind*. Released afterward for charity it became one of the biggest-selling singles of all time.

Diana's brother, the Earl of Spencer, delivered an equally memorable eulogy. He took a swipe at the media and described his sister as "the most hunted woman in the world." He also lashed out at the royal family, saying that his sister "needed no royal title to continue to generate her particular brand of magic."

It was a sentence aimed at the Queen and those who had taken away Diana's right to be styled Her Royal Highness. He further criticized the way of life and traditions of the royals when he pledged to helping William and Harry make their way in life:

> *... on behalf of your mother and sisters, I pledge that we, your blood family, will do all we can to continue the imaginative way in which you were steering these two exceptional young men so that their souls are not simply immersed by duty and tradition but can sing openly as you planned.*

The funeral cortege of Princess Diana makes its way slowly through the streets of London on September 6, 1997.

PART FIVE

A QUEEN FOR THE MILLENNIUM

I cannot lead you into battle. I do not give you laws or administer justice but I can do something else—I can give my heart and my devotion to these old islands and to all the peoples of our brotherhood of nations.

Queen Elizabeth II

CHAPTER 20

A NEW CENTURY DAWNS

Elizabeth made an inauspicious return to duty after Diana's death. In October 1997, in commemoration of the independence of India and the founding of Pakistan fifty years earlier, she set off on a visit to the Indian subcontinent. Robin Cook (1946 – 2005), the British Foreign Minister, had advocated international mediation between India and Pakistan regarding the disputed Kashmir area. The Indian government was offended by his interference, describing the dispute as a purely internal matter.

Just before the tour, the Indian Prime Minister, I.K. Gujral (1919 – 2012) said that the Queen was the leader of a "third rate nation." It was already a nervy trip because she would be visiting Amritsar, scene of the massacre of hundreds of unarmed Indians by British soldiers in 1919. Protestors wanted her to make an apology for the massacre but although she failed to do that, she removed her shoes, laid a wreath and stood silently before the monument commemorating the tragedy.

GOLDEN WEDDING ANNIVERSARY

A happier occasion was to follow, however. On November 20, 1997, she and Prince Philip celebrated their Golden Wedding Anniversary. She was the first monarch in 186 years to reach this milestone and, although the mood was still relatively somber following recent events, it was celebrated in several ways.

Prince Philip gave a speech at Guildhall and on the day itself there was a service of thanksgiving at Westminster Abbey and a celebratory lunch hosted by the Prime Minister. During lunch the Queen paid tribute to her husband, describing him as:

... someone who doesn't take easily to compliments but he has, quite simply, been my strength and stay all these years, and I, and his whole family, and this and many other countries, owe him a debt greater than he would ever claim, or we shall ever know.

THE MODERN MONARCH

December 11, 1997, was a sad day for the Queen and Prince Philip. On that day, the Royal Yacht *Britannia* was decommissioned in Portsmouth. The royal family and courtiers enjoyed a last luncheon in the State Dining Room before saying goodbye to the crew. One of the courtiers reported that the Queen was in tears. Millions watched the quayside service on television. After retiring, *Britannia* became a hugely popular tourist attraction at the Port of Leith near Edinburgh.

The lessons that had to be learned from the death of Diana began to be acted upon. Market research was carried out to gauge modern attitudes to the monarchy and a communications director was employed to polish up the royal brand. It was decided to update some of the old-fashioned public appearances by the royal family. The idea was introduced of themed visits in which the Queen or other members of "the Firm," as Prince Philip called the family, would visit places or take part in events that were all linked.

THE NEVER-ENDING TOUR

The royal overseas visits continued unabated. The Queen, now 72 years of age, embarked on a tour of Brunei and Kuala Lumpur to open the Commonwealth Games with Prince Philip in September 1998. It was a trip supposed to show the monarchy updating itself and allowing the Queen to be more direct and it worked. It was viewed as a great success.

In June 1999, the last of the Queen's children, Prince Edward married Sophie Rhys-Jones (born 1965) at St. George's Chapel, Windsor. Although the ceremony was still broadcast around the world, it was not the lavish occasion of previous royal marriages. The relative austerity seemed somehow appropriate. Edward was appointed Earl of Wessex which went against the tradition of the monarch's male children being created dukes. However, it is anticipated that he will one day inherit the Duke of Edinburgh's title.

GOD SAVE THE JUBILEE

The Queen celebrated her Golden Jubilee in 2002. Intended as a commemoration of her fifty years on the throne, and a chance for her to show her appreciation for the loyalty of her people, the event was marked by celebrations in Britain as well as in many Commonwealth countries. These took place over a period of twelve months and during this time she and her husband also traveled to the Caribbean, Australia, New Zealand, and Canada.

SOPHIE AND THE FAKE SHEIKH

In April 2001, Prince Edward's wife, Sophie, Countess of Wessex was entrapped by *The Sun* journalist, Mahzer Mahmood, the same man who snared the Duchess of York in 2010. Mahmood, posing as an Arab sheikh, secretly taped a meeting with her during which she insulted members of the royal family as well as politicians.

In the course of the conversation, she calls the Queen "old dear" and describes Prime Minister Tony Blair's wife, Cherie (born 1954) as "absolutely horrid, horrid, horrid." She criticizes the politics of Blair and Chancellor of the Exchequer Gordon Brown (born 1951) and cruelly describes the Leader of the Conservative Party, William Hague (born 1961) as "deformed." She says that Prince Charles would marry eventually but not until "the old lady dies," a reference to the Queen Mother.

The Palace fought to clear her name, insisting that the report was "selective, distorted and in several cases, flatly untrue." The Queen and Prince Philip were particularly annoyed that Sophie had broken a royal taboo by straying into the area of politics, strictly off-limits for members of the royal family. Her husband cannot have been too happy either.

Her business partner Murray Harkin, who attended a meeting with the journalist at which the Countess was not present, questioned Edward's sexuality when he said: "There have been rumors for years about Edward. I'm a great believer that there's no smoke without fire."

In 2002, it was announced that the Earl and Countess of Wessex would step aside from their business interests and concentrate on activities and official engagements on behalf of the royal family.

Prince Edward and Sophie, Countess of Wessex at the Trooping the Color parade outside Buckingham Palace, 2013.

Many, especially in the press, had suggested the celebration would be a disappointment. The *Guardian*, for instance, headlined one sniffy piece in February 2002 "God Save the Jubilee." The predictions were proved wrong, however, especially during the actual Jubilee weekend, with fêtes, street parties, and concerts attended by large crowds.

In the end, events that year were only clouded by the deaths of Princess Margaret and the Queen Mother within weeks of each other.

THE TROUBLED PRINCESS

Princess Margaret had been ill for some time and had had part of her left lung removed in 1985 and suffered a mild stroke in 1998. In early 1999, she scalded her feet very badly while taking a bath in her house on the Caribbean island of Mustique. Her mobility was so seriously affected that she started to use a wheelchair and found it difficult to walk unaided.

The year 2001 brought further strokes which left her with partial vision and paralysis on her left side. She was last seen in public at the celebrations for the 101st birthday of the Queen Mother in August 2001 and the 100th birthday celebrations for her aunt, Princess Alice, Duchess of Gloucester in December of that year.

Princess Margaret died in the King Edward VII Hospital in London on February 9, 2002. She was 71 and her sister was by her side. She was buried in a private ceremony, as per her wishes.

THE VIGIL OF THE PRINCES

The Queen Mother kept working almost until the end, fulfilling public engagements in November 2001, at the age of 101. The following month, however, she fell and fractured her pelvis. This did not prevent her from bravely standing for the National Anthem during the memorial service that was held for her husband, George VI, on February 6, 2002,

three days before the death of her daughter, Princess Margaret.

Despite ill health, she attended Margaret's funeral. On March 30, the Queen Mother died in her sleep at Royal Lodge, Windsor Great Park, with her surviving daughter, the Queen, at her bedside. She had lived longer than any member of the royal family in history.

Her coffin lay in state in Westminster Hall and more than 200,000 people came to pay their respects. At one point, Prince Charles, Prince Andrew, Prince Edward and Viscount Linley stood guard at the four corners of the catafalque in the ritual known as the Vigil of the Princes that had only been staged once before, at the lying in state of King George V.

Her funeral route was lined by more than a million people and she was buried beside her husband and younger daughter in St. George's Chapel, Windsor. In a heart-rending gesture, the wreath that had lain on top of her coffin was placed on the Tomb of the Unknown Warrior in Westminster Abbey. She had done the same thing on her wedding day in 1923.

THE MOST MAGICAL GRANDMOTHER

The Queen was, of course deeply saddened by these events, and touched by the sympathy shown to her. On the night before her mother's funeral, she paid tribute to her on television in a short address. She talked about the loss she felt and thanked the nation for "the outpouring of affection which has accompanied her death." She spoke of being "overwhelmed."

It was the type of emotion that would not have been shown some years previously and part of a series of expressions of human emotion that the royal family was demonstrating. Prince Charles had also appeared on television, speaking of "the most magical grandmother you could possibly have." He described how he would "miss her laugh and wonderful wisdom born of so much experience and an innate sensitivity to life." Even the young Princes,

HER MAJESTY QUEEN ELIZABETH
THE QUEEN MOTHER

Queen Elizabeth The Queen Mother (1900 – 2002) was the mother of Queen Elizabeth II, and the wife of King George VI. She was Queen of the United Kingdom and the Dominions from her husband's accession in 1936 until his death in 1952. She was the last Empress of India.

William and Harry, gave interviews about their great grandmother.

But it was hard for the Queen; it gave her what her friend Margaret Rhodes described as "a terrible wallop of grief." These were the two people with whom she talked every day, on the telephone if not in person. Such a loss would take their toll but she returned to her duties, as ever, encouraged by a new connection with her subjects.

APPROACHING OLD AGE

Queen Elizabeth's health has always been robust but in January 2003, while visiting the stables at Sandringham, she slipped, tearing a cartilage in her right knee. It required surgery and she was immobilized for some time, unable to go out for walks in the countryside or ride. A year later, she underwent the same procedure. Age was catching up with her as evidenced by the fact that she now rode fell ponies and not the large horses that she had ridden most of her life.

With her mother and sister now gone, she sought companionship with her cousin Margaret Rhodes (1925 – 2016) who had been a lady-in-waiting to the Queen Mother from 1991 to 2002 and lived in a grace and favor residence, the Garden House, in Windsor Great Park. After church on Sunday, the Queen could be found enjoying her favorite tipple, gin and Dubonnet in the company of Margaret Rhodes until Mrs. Rhodes passed away in November 2016.

The Queen's beloved confidante, Bobo MacDonald had died in her suite at Buckingham Palace in 1993, but her role was taken to some extent in 2002 by Angela Kelly, a designer, dressmaker and milliner, who is twenty-five years younger than Her Majesty. Kelly liked to call herself "personal assistant." She has become a trusted confidante of the Queen and is always with her.

Angela Kelly

Often described as the Queen's "gatekeeper," Angela Kelly has been personal assistant to the Queen since 2002. Born in Walton, Merseyside, in 1952, she is the daughter of a crane driver and a nurse, and is always with the Queen. In terms of Elizabeth's wardrobe, she is highly attentive to the situations in which the Queen will be placed, adopting an almost theatrical approach to what she wears.

She approaches the royal wardrobe with a meticulous eye for detail, even researching at the venues she will visit on foreign and domestic tours to establish colors and styles. As one royal insider said: "Angela understands the Queen needs to wear something that sets her apart from the crowd when she is at a distance, and that inside she can wear beige and grey, things that are more neutral."

Kelly uses the talents of new couturiers but also designs a great many of the Queen's outfits herself. Importantly, she has created computerized inventories of the Queen's large private jewelry collection which allows her to select pieces from which the Queen can choose. The Queen enjoys her company and often when the two are together, the sound of laughter can be heard echoing down the Palace corridors.

THE QUEEN'S COATS OF MANY COLORS

Royal observers have long recognized that there is a strict dress code etiquette for the Queen and other close members of the royal family. Hats, gloves, tiaras—all have rules stipulating when they are worn and by whom. Even Prince George, son of the Duke and Duchess of Cambridge, has to adhere to a dress code that always sees him wearing a smart pair of shorts and a formal shirt, and he is unlikely ever to be seen in a Batman tee-shirt like other little boys his age.

Experts in English etiquette insist that ladies should always wear hats for formal events and the Queen has never disappointed, always seen in colorful and bold headgear during official engagements. The hats are always color-coordinated with the brightly colored coats she wears. Angela Kelly, Her Majesty's personal assistant, is said to be responsible for these coats of many colors, but the Queen has said: "If I wore beige, nobody would know who I am."

The bright colors also, however, make it easier for members of the public to see her through the throngs of people who turn up at engagements to catch a glimpse of her. The etiquette experts also advocate the wearing of gloves for ladies but for the Queen there is also a practical reason. She shakes the hands of so many people on a royal visit that her gloves serve as a protection from germs being passed to her.

As for tiaras, they are worn only by married ladies and only at night. They indicate to everyone at a ball or banquet that a lady wearing a tiara is already taken and serves as a warning to men not to make advances towards that particular lady.

The Queen's bright green outfit means she can be clearly seen from a distance by members of the public among the large men in military uniforms of the Band of the Blues and Royals.

A FOOTMAN FROM THE
DAILY MIRROR

In the modern age of media intrusion, the royal family is a popular target. On November 19, 2003, the Queen awoke to a disturbing headline in the *Daily Mirror*. The front page heralded a "World Exclusive" and bore a photograph of a royal footman standing on the well-known Buckingham Palace balcony with the word "INTRUDER" printed in red above his head.

A headline shouted: *"As Bush arrives, We Reveal Mirrorman Has Been a Palace Footman for Two Months In The Biggest Royal Security Scandal Ever."* Fourteen of the paper's inside pages carried photographs taken inside the Palace. The royal family's daily routines were described and sensational headlines such as *"I Could Have Poisoned the Queen"* were thrown in for good measure.

A *Daily Mirror* reporter, Ryan Parry had fraudulently obtained a position as a footman. This came just a month after a hoaxer named Aaron Barschak succeeded in gatecrashing Prince William's twenty-first birthday party. Worst of all, however, Parry's exposé came a day before US President George W. Bush's state visit to Britain and to Buckingham Palace.

The piece described the use of bad language at the Palace, such as Princess Anne using the F-word and Prince Edward swearing at a footman. One photograph that caught the eye depicted the Queen's breakfast table with its crisp, white linen, silver cutlery, and fine bone china alongside a rather cheap-looking transistor radio and three Tupperware boxes from which the royal breakfast cereal could be dispensed.

The *Mirror* tried to express the article in terms of highlighting the lax security at Buckingham Palace but it was, in reality, tawdry voyeurism. The story and the photographs continued the following day. The Queen was naturally furious.

Legal action was taken and an injunction was obtained, preventing the newspaper from further publication of Ryan Parry's photos and experiences. The photographs were returned to the Palace.

President Bush's visit went ahead, in the middle of huge security and demonstrations against the war in Iraq. George Bush later recalled that the Queen "was unruffled by the protests. She had seen a lot during her life, and it didn't seem to faze her."

The Queen and President George W. Bush.

CHAPTER 21

LINES OF SUCCESSION

CHARLES MARRIES CAMILLA

There had been endless speculation about Mrs. Camilla Parker-Bowles and Prince Charles and the formalization of their relationship was finally announced on February 10, 2005. The Queen's consent under the Royal Marriages Act of 1772 was obtained and she and her husband congratulated the couple.

The wedding took place on April 9 that year at Windsor Guildhall with a civil service followed by religious prayer. The Prince was the first member of the royal family to marry in a civil ceremony and this style of marriage was probably chosen to avoid the controversy that a church wedding would have created, given that they were both divorcees and Charles was the future Supreme Governor of the Church of England.

The ceremony was not attended by the Queen but she did attend the blessing and the reception that followed. It was said at the time that Charles and Camilla wanted the ceremony to be as low-key as possible and that the presence of the monarch would elevate it into an entirely different type of occasion. The initial date for the ceremony had to be changed following the death of Pope John Paul II (1920 – 2005). Prince Charles had to attend his funeral first.

The Prince of Wales and Mrs. Camilla Parker-Bowles at Birkhall in Scotland after announcing that they were to marry in April 2005.

THE DUCHESS OF CORNWALL

Some respect for the late Princess Diana was shown when it was announced that Camilla would never be the Princess of Wales. She would be named the Duchess of Cornwall, a title taken from Charles's ducal titles. She had never been popular with the public, and was seen as having contributed to the troubles of the beloved Diana. But the warmth shown to her by Princes William and Harry went some way to gaining her more approval from the British public.

As Queen Elizabeth reached the age of 80 in April 2006, everything was calm. Prince Charles appeared on television, praising his "darling mama" and there was a dinner for twenty-five members of the royal family at Kew Palace. The table plan sat Elizabeth between Prince Charles and Prince William. The Duke of Edinburgh was now 85 years old but showed no signs of easing up on his duties.

PRINCE WILLIAM AND HIS GRANNY

Prince William attended St. Andrews University, graduating in 2005. He wanted, like his younger brother Harry, to join the military but he would later have responsibilities for managing what were at present his father's estates. Therefore, he took a year out to work on Prince Charles's Gloucestershire farm as well as at Chatsworth, owned by the Duke and Duchess of Devonshire. At the beginning of 2006, he enrolled at Sandhurst Military College to embark on his military career.

Elizabeth was an important influence on him, as she was with all of her grandchildren. William was, of course, special because of his unique position as second in line to the throne. While he had been at Eton, he would often pop down the road to Windsor Castle to have tea with his granny. He said of her:

Two future kings, Prince William and Prince Charles, with Prince Harry.

> *She's a real role model. She's just very helpful on any sort of difficulties or problems I might be having. But I'm quite a private person as well, so I don't really talk that much about what I sort of feel or think.*

MEETING CATHERINE MIDDLETON

While at St. Andrews, William met Catherine Middleton (born 1982) who lived in the same residence as he did—St. Salvator's Hall. They began dating in 2003 but by 2005, Kate, as she became popularly known, was complaining to her lawyer about harassment by the media. The couple broke up in April 2007 but the relationship was resumed shortly after.

They became engaged in October 2010 while they were on a ten-day holiday in Kenya to celebrate William passing his helicopter search and rescue course. The engagement ring was the one worn by William's late mother, Princess Diana.

Their marriage took place on April 29, 2011, at Westminster Abbey, the service conducted by the Archbishop of Canterbury, Rowan Williams (born 1950) and with Prince Harry as best man. Pippa (born 1983), Catherine's sister was maid of honor. William is not heir apparent to the throne and, therefore, the wedding was not a state occasion, but attendees included foreign royalty, heads of state and celebrities.

THE FUTURE QUEEN

The day was declared a public holiday in the United Kingdom. Before the service, the Queen conferred on Prince William the titles of Duke of Cambridge, Earl of Strathearn, and Baron Carrickfergus. On marrying the Prince, Catherine became Her Royal Highness the Duchess of Cambridge.

Catherine Middleton is an exemplar of how the Queen and the royal family had moved on from the days of Diana. Back then, in finding a spouse for the heir to the throne, the emphasis had been on finding a woman with no sexual history and no skeletons in the family cupboard.

In Catherine Middleton, however, they took on a young woman who was up to the job of being a member of the royal family and, one day, the future Queen. It is also thought that her wedding and the hysteria surrounding it has led to a resurgence in popularity for the monarchy.

A GESTURE OF RECONCILIATION

The Queen has visited an astonishing 116 nations during her reign, some of them on multiple occasions. One country she had not visited, however, was the Republic of Ireland. At the age of 85, she finally did so, in May 2011. It was the first royal visit to the Republic since the battle for Irish independence that had been fought during the reign of her grandfather George V. In fact, the last visit by a British monarch was 1911.

Naturally, security had to be extremely tight as Republican feelings still ran high in certain quarters, but Her Majesty carried off a difficult four days with great aplomb and dignity. She managed to speak a little Gaelic, noticeably wore emerald green and she bowed somberly in front of a memorial to those who had lost their lives in the fight for Irish independence against the British.

As a gesture of reconciliation and friendship, it was a resounding success. She memorably said at a state banquet at Dublin Castle:

> *To all those who have suffered as a consequence of our troubled past, I extend my sincere thoughts and deep sympathy. With the benefit of historical hindsight, we can see things which we wish we had done differently or not at all.*

IMPORTANT PROPOSALS

Queen Elizabeth's reign has been filled with historic changes and memorable firsts. One significant change came in 2011 at the 22nd

Catherine Middleton

The future Queen of Great Britain and the Commonwealth, Catherine Elizabeth "Kate" Middleton was born on January 9, 1982, in Chapel Row, a village in Berkshire, into an upper-middle-class family.

She is the oldest of three children born to Michael Middleton (born 1949) who worked for British Airways, and his wife Carol (born 1955) who had been a British Airways flight despatcher and flight attendant. Michael Middleton's family has ties with British aristocracy.

The couple have two other children, Pippa (born 1983) and James (born 1987). After being based in Amman, Jordan for two years, the Middletons returned to Britain and in 1987, started the party supply company, Party Pieces. Catherine boarded at Marlborough College before going to study at St. Andrews University where she met her future husband, Prince William.

After obtaining an MA in the history of art, she became a buyer for the retail clothing chain Jigsaw, working part-time until November 2007 when she began working for her parents' company, with responsibilities for catalog design and production, as well as marketing and photography. She married Prince William in 2011 and the couple have two children, Prince George (born 2013) who is third in line of succession to the Queen, and Princess Charlotte (born 2015) who is fourth in line of succession.

Commonwealth Heads of Government Meeting in Australia. The meeting agreed to important proposals put forward by British Prime Minister David Cameron regarding changes in line of succession to the throne.

These proposals demonstrated beyond all doubt that the Queen and the royal family were becoming more progressive in their thinking and that they were more finely attuned to their times than perhaps in the past. The changes meant that male preference primogeniture would be replaced by absolute primogeniture for all persons in line of succession born after October 28, 2011.

In other words, a daughter of a monarch would not be superseded in line of succession by a younger brother. The ban on a monarch marrying a Catholic was to be lifted and the requirement of the sovereign's permission to marry was to be limited to the first six people in line of succession to the throne.

A NEW DIRECT HEIR

A new arrival in the line of succession generated global media coverage on July 22, 2013, when the Duke and Duchess of Cambridge's first child, George Alexander Louis of Cambridge, was born at St. Mary's Hospital, Paddington. For the first time since 1894, there were now three direct heirs to the British throne.

In such unusual circumstances, Her Majesty had ensured that Prince George would enjoy the title Royal Highness by overturning the Letters Patent by King George V that had been gazetted in 1917. King George's wish was that the term "Royal Highness" and the titular dignity "Prince" or "Princess" should be restricted to the children of the sovereign, the children of the sons of the sovereign and the eldest living son of a Prince of Wales.

In 2013, the Succession to the Throne Act brought further modernization to the monarchy, in accordance with the decision made at the 2011 Commonwealth Heads Meeting in Australia, stipulating that from now on the first child born to a monarch or heir to the throne would become sovereign regardless of sex.

Although Prince George was born first, the Act does benefit Princess Charlotte Elizabeth Diana who was born to the Duke and Duchess of Cambridge on May 2, 2015. She will remain fourth in line, even if her parents have any more sons.

IN THE EVENT OF THE QUEEN'S DEATH

The moment the Queen's Private Secretary utters the code words "London Bridge is down" to the Prime Minister will be a sad one for the nation and the Commonwealth because it will signal the death of Elizabeth II.

There are careful plans for events following such news. After the Prime Minister has been informed, the leaders of the 32 Commonwealth countries for which she is sovereign will be told. The bad news will be passed to the media after these leaders have been told. Programs on BBC1, 2 and 4 will be interrupted and these stations will switch to the News, as will BBC Radios 4 and 5 Live.

Both Houses of Parliament will be recalled and twelve days of mourning will begin. The Queen will lie in state in Westminster Hall for four days and it is estimated that more than half a million people will troop past her catafalque.

Her funeral will take place twelve days after her death and her body will then be taken by road to Windsor Castle where she will be interred in the Royal Vault. On her death, Prince Charles will become King Charles III.

LONG MAY SHE REIGN

In December 2007, the Queen became the longest-lived British monarch, surpassing her great-great-grandmother, Queen Victoria. On September 9, 2015, she became the longest-reigning British monarch. She has currently chalked up 65 years on the throne, Victoria having occupied it for 63 years and 216 days.

She is the longest-reigning queen regnant in history and is the world's oldest reigning monarch. Following the death of King Bhumibol (1927 – 2016) of Thailand in 2016, she became the world's longest-serving current head of state. On February 6, 2017, she became the first British King or Queen to celebrate a Sapphire Jubilee.

But age was finally beginning to catch up with the Duke of Edinburgh. In May 2017, a month before his 96th birthday, Buckingham Palace announced that he would be retiring from royal duties the following fall. He had carried out 110 days of engagements the previous year and remains patron, president or member of more than 780 organizations and although he will continue his association with them, he "will no longer play an active role by attending engagements."

SERVICE, SACRIFICE, AND DUTY

What about the Queen? In 2013, when Queen Beatrix of Holland (born 1938) and Albert II of Belgium (born 1934) decided to abdicate within months of each other, the ongoing speculation as to whether Elizabeth would consider a similar move in favor of Prince Charles increased. The 2014 abdication of the Spanish King Juan Carlos (born 1938) gave rise to further conjecture.

There is no doubt she has reduced her workload, and now refrains from long-distance travel. Prince Charles has ably begun to step in where he can, representing his mother. In November 2013, he attended the Commonwealth Head of Government Meeting in Sri Lanka in her place.

It was the first such meeting the Queen had missed since 1971, when Prime Minister Edward Heath had advised her not to attend due to the apartheid crisis in South Africa. Nonetheless, she made it to the 2015 meeting in Malta.

It has to be drawn from all of this that the Queen, a woman steeped in service, sacrifice and duty, would only consider abdication if she was unable to do the job that she was born into. At 91, she seems fit and healthy and it looks like it may be some time yet before she hands over the reins to her successors.

The British royal family gather on the balcony of Buckingham Palace to celebrate Queen Elizabeth's 90th birthday, June 2016.

Her Majesty Queen Elizabeth II,
after her Coronation in 1953.

CHAPTER 22

THE QUEEN IN POPULAR CULTURE

THE QUEEN AT THE MOVIES

The Queen has been portrayed numerous times in films and television dramas and comedies over the years but the first depiction of her was, indeed, a strange one. Steve Walden in drag, played her in the X-rated *Tricia's Wedding* (1971), a spoof of the wedding of President Richard Nixon's daughter, Tricia.

In 1975, Huguette Funfrock, a French actress who is famous for her resemblance to the Queen, appeared in the James Bond parody, *Bons Baisers de Hong Kong,* that also starred Mickey Rooney as well as Bernard Lee and Lois Maxwell who had appeared in the real Bond movies. Funfrock also played her in *Le Bourreau des Coeurs* (1983) and *Aces Go Places 3* (1984).

Another actress who specializes in playing the Queen is the now-retired English actress, Jeannette Charles. She played her in many films including *Queen Kong* (1976), The Rutles' movie *All You Need is Cash* (1978), *National Lampoon's European Vacation* (1985), *The Naked Gun: From the Files of Police Squad!* (1988) and *Austin Powers in Goldmember* (2002). She has also appeared on *Saturday Night Live* and *Big Brother*.

Prunella Scales played the Queen in Rowan Atkinson's spy spoof, *Johnny English* in 2003 and Neve Campbell portrayed her in another spoof, *Churchill: The Hollywood Years* in 2004.

The actress who has probably been most celebrated for playing Her Majesty, however, is Helen Mirren who has played her both on screen and on stage. On film, she won an Oscar and a BAFTA for her performance as Elizabeth in *The Queen* (2006). Stephen Frears' hugely successful film of Peter Morgan's screenplay depicts the royal family's response to the death of Diana, Princess of Wales. After the film was shown at the Venice Film Festival, Mirren received a five-minute standing ovation.

In another Oscar-winning film, *The King's Speech*, in which Colin Firth plays George VI struggling with his speech impediment,

venezia 63
competizione

OFFICAL SELECTION
VENICE FILM FESTIVAL 2006

QUEEN OF A NATION, QUEEN OF HEARTS.

HELEN MIRREN

THE QUEEN

A FILM BY STEPHEN FREARS

IN CINEMAS SOON

Movie poster for *The Queen* (2006) starring Helen Mirren.

11-year-old Freya Wilson powerfully plays the young Princess Elizabeth. She said that she had studied the Princess by listening to clips of her speeches.

Princess Elizabeth's escape with friends from Buckingham Palace on VE Day is liberally fictionalized in the romantic comedy-drama film *A Royal Night Out*. In the film each girl is given an army officer chaperone and instructed to be back at the Palace by 1 a.m. Margaret quickly becomes bored and escapes the attentions of her escort and Elizabeth, played by Sarah Gadon, does the same shortly after. Margaret meets a naval officer and is led into nightclubs, gambling dens, and brothels, while Elizabeth meets an airman who is AWOL and has her own adventures while trying to locate her sister. Needless to say, they do not make it back to the Palace by their deadline.

Jennifer Saunders memorably voiced the Queen in the 2015 animation, *Minions*, a spin-off from the *Despicable Me* franchise and Penelope Wilton donned the fictional crown in the 2016 version of Roald Dahl's *The BFG* that starred Mark Rylance as the Big Friendly Giant.

THE QUEEN ON TELEVISION

Queen Elizabeth has appeared as a character in too many television shows to list here. She has featured in such shows as *The Simpsons*, *Family Guy*, *Saturday Night Live*, and *Doctor Who*.

Huguette Funfrock and Jeannette Charles appeared in numerous television comedy shows from the 1970s onward, but the Queen has been portrayed on the small screen by many other actors and comedians. Scottish comedian Stanley Baxter's *The Many Faces of Stanley Baxter* often featured him performing his impressions of famous people and, somewhat controversially, the Queen did not escape, known in his shows as "the Duchess of Brendagh."

American actress and comedienne, Carol Burnett portrayed the Queen memorably with a posh, high-pitched voice in several sketches on her hugely successful *The Carol Burnett Show* and before the War of the Waleses broke out, Margaret Tyzack played the Queen in the syrupy 1982 television film, *Charles & Diana: A Royal Love Story*, a dramatization of the courtship and wedding of the royal couple. Prince Charles was played by David Robb and Caroline Bliss took on the role of Lady Diana Spencer. Somewhat astonishingly, Christopher Lee, the doyen of the horror film, played Prince Philip. This was the first TV movie ever made about Diana.

In the same week as *Charles & Diana: A Royal Love Story* was aired, so too was *The Royal Romance of Charles and Diana*, which with its stellar cast, was altogether more successful. The Queen was played this time by Dana Wynter, star of the cult movie *Invasion of the Body Snatchers*. Catherine Oxenberg played Diana, while Christopher Baines was Prince Charles. Olivia de Havilland played the Queen Mother and Stewart Granger was the Duke of Edinburgh.

Alan Bennett's play *A Question of Attribution*, about Soviet spy and Surveyor of the Queen's Pictures Anthony Blunt, was turned into a BBC drama in 1991 with Prunella Scales wonderfully cast in the role of Queen Elizabeth II.

Diana: Her True Story of 1993 was a television film based on Andrew Morton's notorious book of the same name. Anne Stallybrass played the Queen and Kristin Scott Thomas's younger sister, Serena, played Diana.

Elizabeth Richard first played the Queen in the TV movie *Giving Tongue* in 1996 and has gone on to portray Her Majesty a number of times—in *Gobble* (1997), *Harry Hill* (2000), *The Nick Cannon Show* (2002), *What a Girl Wants* (2003), *Never Say Never Mind: The Swedish Bikini Team* (2003), and the movie *2012* (2009).

Another serial portrayer of the Queen is Rosemary Leach who has played her in the controversial 2002 American TV movie *Prince*

William in which the son of the singer Lulu, Jordan Frieda, played the Prince and in the 2006 BBC comedy drama *Tea with Betty* in which Her Majesty turns up on a municipal council estate to have tea with a resident. Rosemary Leach reprised her characterization of Elizabeth for the 2009 television film about Margaret Thatcher, *Margaret*.

Also made in 2009, *The Queen* was an ABC docudrama that showed Elizabeth II at different points in her life, the Queen played by a different actress in each of five episodes. The actresses involved were Emilia Fox who played her at the time of Princess Margaret's relationship with Peter Townsend; Samantha Bond during the early 1970s and at the time of the attempted kidnap of Princess Anne; Susan Jameson during the 1986 Commonwealth Games in Edinburgh at the time of a boycott by many Commonwealth nations in protest at the Thatcher government's policy of maintaining sporting links with South Africa; Barbara Flynn portrayed the Queen during the *"Annus Horribilis"* of 1992; and Diana Quick at the time of the marriage of Prince Charles and Camilla Parker-Bowles.

The 2011 American TV movie, *William & Catherine: A Royal Romance* featured Jane Alexander as William's grandmother and Emma Thompson played her in *Walking the Dogs* (2012). This comedy drama was based on the Michael Fagan incident of 1982.

The most recent portrayal of Her Majesty was in 2016's Netflix series *The Crown*, a biographical story of Elizabeth's reign. Claire Foy plays the Queen and former Doctor Who Matt Smith is the Duke of Edinburgh. This series has been praised for the quality of the performances—especially those of Foy and John Lithgow as Winston Churchill—as well as for its historical accuracy. The producers plan to cover the entire reign of Her Majesty in ensuing seasons starting in December 2017.

The Crown (2016) Netflix TV series starring Claire Foy as the Queen and Matt Smith as Prince Philip.

THE QUEEN ON THE STAGE

The Queen has been portrayed in a number of productions for the stage. As in the televised version, Prunella Scales played the Queen in Alan Bennett's *A Question of Attribution*, about Anthony Blunt. The 2013 play, *Handbagged*, by Moira Buffini looked at the relationship between Prime Minister Margaret Thatcher and the Queen. Two actresses took the role of Her Majesty—Lucy Robinson when she was younger and Marion Bailey when she was older. After opening at the Tricycle Theater in Kilburn in north London, it ran very successfully in London's West End in 2014.

Helen Mirren reprised her role as Elizabeth in 2013 in the stage play *The Audience*, written by Peter Morgan who also wrote the film *The Queen*. It deals with the weekly audiences given by Her Majesty to her prime ministers. Only Harold Macmillan, Lord Home and Edward Heath are omitted. Tony Blair replaced James Callaghan when it transferred to Broadway in 2015.

King Charles III is Mike Bartlett's 2014 popular stage production that imagines the first days of Charles' ascension to the throne following the Queen's death and features a future version of the royal family who are at loggerheads with each other.

It includes many controversial scenes that depict the Queen's funeral, a ghostly apparition of the late Princess Diana, and a furious Camilla Parker-Bowles slapping her stepson Prince William, who is at war with his father. Meanwhile the Duchess Of Cambridge is portrayed as scheming and "Lady Macbeth-like."

THE QUEEN IN FICTION

SAVING THE QUEEN
BY WILLIAM F. BUCKLEY (1976)

The Queen's life is threatened and only one man can save her—Blackford Oakes, a deep-cover agent of the CIA. The first in Buckley's series featuring this character.

THE UNCOMMON READER
BY ALAN BENNETT (2007)

While in pursuit of her corgis who have wandered off, the Queen finds a mobile library and decides to borrow a book. She is helped by a young man from the Buckingham Palace kitchen and as she looks for the tome of her choice, she is transformed by the magic of the written word. In his customarily masterful way, Bennett reveals how the power of literature can affect the life of even the most uncommon reader.

THE QUEEN AND I
BY SUE TOWNSEND (1993)

When a new British government confiscates all royal properties, the royals find themselves evicted and being forced to live in a council house and suffer indignities such as having to line up at a supermarket checkout. This outrageous novel by the creator of Adrian Mole was a number one bestseller. Townsend followed up with a 2006 sequel, *Queen Camilla*.

THE AUTOBIOGRAPHY OF THE QUEEN
BY EMMA TENNANT (2008)

The Queen disappears from Balmoral and heads for St. Lucia in the Caribbean where she has bought a house to retire to. Here, posing as Gloria Smith, she intends to write her autobiography. The house, however, has not been built and she is reduced to fending for herself, something she has never experienced. In this funny and touching story the Queen is reminded of how much she needs her subjects and how much they need her.

MRS. QUEEN TAKES A TRAIN
BY WILLIAM KUHN (2012)

Bored, the Queen walks out of the Palace and goes off in search of fun, leaving her courtiers exasperated as they search for her before anyone finds out and scandal erupts.

CHAPTER 23

A TIMELINE OF THE REIGN OF QUEEN ELIZABETH II

1952 Elizabeth receives news of the death of her father, King George VI, while in a remote part of Kenya. She flies back to Britain as Queen. She declares that Windsor would continue as the name of the royal house.

1953 The Coronation of Queen Elizabeth II at Westminster Abbey. She visits Bermuda, Fiji, Jamaica, Panama, and Tonga. Queen Mary dies.

1954 The Queen visits Aden, Australia, Ceylon, Cocos Islands, Gibraltar, Libya, Malta, New Zealand and Uganda.

1955 The Queen visits Norway. Princess Margaret announces she will not marry Group Captain Peter Townsend. Anthony Eden becomes Prime Minister.

1956 The Queen visits Nigeria and Sweden.

1957 The Queen visits Canada, France, Denmark, Portugal and the United States. Harold Macmillan becomes Prime Minister. On her visit to the United States, she addresses the United Nations on behalf of the Commonwealth.

1958 The Queen visits the Netherlands.

1959 The Queen visits Canada and the United States.

1960 Birth of her third child, Prince Andrew. The name Mountbatten-Windsor is adopted for male-line descendants of Elizabeth and Philip who do not have royal titles. Princess Margaret marries Antony Armstrong-Jones.

1961 The Queen visits Cyprus, Gambia, Ghana, India, Iran, Italy, Nepal, Liberia, Pakistan, Sierra Leone and Vatican City.

1963 The Queen visits Canada, Fiji, New Zealand and Australia. Lord Home becomes Prime Minister.

1964 The Queen visits Canada. Birth of her fourth child, Prince Edward. Harold Wilson becomes Prime Minister.

1965 The Queen visits Ethiopia, Sudan, West Berlin and West Germany. Death of Winston Churchill.

1966 The Queen visits Antigua, Bahamas, Barbados, British Guiana, British Virgin Islands, Belgium, Dominica, Grenada, Jamaica, Montserrat, Saint Christopher-Nevis-Anguilla, Saint Lucia, Saint Vincent and the Grenadines, Trinidad and Tobago, and Turks and Cacos Islands.

1967 The Queen visits Malta and Canada.

1968 The Queen visits Brazil and Chile.

1969 The Queen visits Austria.

1970 The Queen visits Australia, Canada, Fiji, New Zealand, and Tonga. Edward Heath becomes Prime Minister. In Australia, she undertakes her first-ever walkabout.

1971 The Queen visits Canada and Turkey.

1972 The Queen visits Brunei, France, Kenya, Malaysia, Mauritius, Seychelles, Singapore, Thailand, the Maldives, and Yugoslavia.

1973 The Queen visits Australia, Canada and Fiji. Princess Anne marries Captain Mark Phillips.

1974 The Queen visits Australia, Cook Islands, Indonesia, New Hebrides, New Zealand, Norfolk Island, Papua New Guinea, and Solomon Islands. Harold Wilson again becomes Prime Minister.

1975 The Queen visits Bahamas, Barbados, Bermuda, Hong Kong, Jamaica, Japan, and Mexico.

1976 The Queen visits Canada, Finland, Luxembourg, and the United States. She opens the 1976 Summer Olympics in Montreal, Canada. James Callaghan becomes Prime Minister.

1977 The Queen's Silver Jubilee, marking 25 years on the throne. She visits Antigua and Barbuda, Australia, Bahamas, Barbados, British Virgin Islands, Canada, Fiji, New Zealand, Papua New Guinea, Tonga, and Western Samoa. Princess Anne's son Peter Phillips is born.

1978 The Queen visits Canada, West Berlin, and West Germany.

1979 The Queen visits Bahrain, Botswana, Denmark, Kuwait, Malawi, Oman, Saudi Arabia, Tanzania, Qatar, United Arab Emirates, and Zambia. Anthony Blunt, Surveyor of the Queen's Pictures, is exposed as a Soviet spy. Margaret Thatcher becomes Prime Minister.

1980 The Queen visits Algeria, Australia, Italy, Morocco, Switzerland, Tunisia, and Vatican City. The Queen plays an important role in Zimbabwe joining the Commonwealth, after being granted independence by the United Kingdom.

1981 Prince Charles marries Lady Diana Spencer at St. Paul's Cathedral. The Queen visits Australia, Canada, New Zealand, Norway, and Sri Lanka. Princess Anne's daughter Zara Phillips is born.

1982 The passing of the Canada Act brings an end to British executive authority in Canada, but preserves the monarchy. Prince William is born. Catherine Middleton is born. The Queen visits Australia, Fiji, Kiribati, Nauru, Papua New Guinea, Solomon Islands, and Tuvalu. Prince Andrew serves in the Falklands War.

1983 The Queen visits Bangladesh, Bermuda, Canada, Cayman Islands, Cyprus, Jamaica, India, Kenya, Mexico, Sweden, and the United States.

1984 Prince Harry is born. The Queen visits Canada, Cyprus, and Jordan.

1985 The Queen visits Antigua and Barbuda, Bahamas, Barbados, Belize, Dominica, Grenada, Inagua, Portugal, Saint Kitts and Nevis, Saint Lucia, Saint Vincent and the Grenadines, Trinidad and Tobago.

1986 The Queen celebrates her 60th birthday and visits Australia, China, Hong Kong, Nepal, and New Zealand. Prince Andrew marries Sarah Ferguson.

1987 The Queen visits Canada and West Germany.

1988 The Queen visits Australia, the Netherlands, and Spain. Prince Andrew's daughter Princess Beatrice is born.

1989 The Queen visits Barbados, Malaysia, and Singapore.

1990 The Queen visits Canada, Germany, Iceland, and New Zealand. John Major becomes Prime Minister. Prince Andrew's daughter Princess Eugenie is born.

1991 The Queen visits Kenya, Namibia, the United States, and Zimbabwe. She is the first British monarch to address a joint meeting of the United States Congress.

1992 The Queen endures her "*Annus Horribilis.*" She visits Australia, Canada, France, Germany and Malta. The Prince of Wales and Diana, Princess of Wales separate. Prince Andrew and Sarah Ferguson separate. Princess Anne divorces Captain Mark Phillips and marries Commander Timothy Laurence. Parts of Windsor Castle are destroyed by fire.

1993 The Queen visits Belgium, Cyprus, and Hungary. She begins paying income tax.

1994 The Queen visits Anguilla, Bahamas, Belize, Bermuda, Canada, Cayman Islands, Dominica, France, Guyana, Jamaica, and Russia.

1995 The Queen visits New Zealand, and South Africa. She writes to Charles and Diana recommending that they divorce.

1996 The Queen visits the Czech Republic, Poland, and Thailand.

1997 Diana, Princess of Wales dies in a car crash in Paris. The Queen and the Duke of Edinburgh celebrate their Golden Wedding. She visits Canada, India, and Pakistan. Tony Blair becomes Prime Minister.

1998 The Queen visits Belgium, Brunei, and Malaysia.

1999 The Queen visits Ghana, Mozambique, South Africa, and South Korea. Prince Edward marries Sophie Rhys-Jones.

2000 The Queen visits Australia, Italy, and Vatican City.

2001 The Queen visits Norway.

2002 The deaths of Princess Margaret and Queen Elizabeth, the Queen Mother. The Queen celebrates her Golden Jubilee. She visits Australia, Canada, New Zealand, and Jamaica

2003 The Queen visits Nigeria. Prince Edward's daughter Lady Louise Windsor is born.

2004 The Queen visits France and Germany.

2005 The Queen visits Canada and Malta. Prince Charles marries Camilla Parker-Bowles.

2006 The Queen celebrates her 80th birthday and visits Australia, Estonia, Latvia, Lithuania, and Singapore.

2007 The Queen becomes the longest-living British monarch. She visits Belgium, Malta, the Netherlands, Uganda, and the United States. The Queen and the Duke of Edinburgh celebrate their 60th wedding anniversary. Prince Edward's son James, Viscount Severn is born. Gordon Brown becomes Prime Minister.

2008 The Queen visits Slovakia, Slovenia, and Turkey.

2009 The Queen visits Bermuda, and Trinidad and Tobago.

2010 The Queen visits Canada, Oman, and United Arab Emirates. She addresses the United Nations for a second time. David Cameron becomes Prime Minister.

2011 The Queen visits Australia and Ireland. Prince William marries Catherine Middleton and they become the Duke and Duchess of Cambridge.

2012 The Queen celebrates her Diamond Jubilee, 60 years on the throne.

2013 Prince George is born to the Duke and Duchess of Cambridge. He is third in line to the throne.

2014 The Queen visits France, Italy, and Vatican City.

2015 The Queen becomes the United Kingdom's longest-serving monarch. She visits Germany and Malta. Princess Charlotte is born to the Duke and Duchess of Cambridge.

2016 Theresa May becomes Prime Minister.

2017 The Duke of Edinburgh retires from some public duties.

Her Majesty Queen Elizabeth II at
Buckingham Palace, April 4, 1953.

FURTHER READING

This popular biography of Queen Elizabeth II is designed to be an informative and entertaining introductory text. There are many more academic publications available should the reader wish to delve more deeply. Publications that were especially useful during the preparation of this book are listed below, and contemporary newspaper and magazine articles are cited at the point where they appear within the text.

Bedell Smith, Sally, *Elizabeth the Queen: The Life of a Modern Monarch*. New York, Random House, 2012.

Bedell Smith, Sally, *Prince Charles: The Misunderstood Prince*. London, Michael Joseph, 2017.

Bradford, Sarah, *George VI: The Dutiful King*. London, Penguin, 2002.

Bradford, Sarah, *Queen Elizabeth II: Her Life in Our Times*. New York, Viking, 2012.

Brandreth, Gyles, *Philip and Elizabeth: Portrait of a Marriage*. New York, W.W. Norton, 2004.

Burgess, Major Colin, *Behind Palace Doors*. London, John Blake, 2007.

Crawford, Marion, *The Little Princesses*. First published 1950. London, Orion, republished 2003.

Dalrymple, William & Anand, Anita, *Koh-i-Noor: The History of the World's Most Infamous Diamond*. London, Bloomsbury Publishing, 2017.

Dimbleby, Jonathan, *The Prince of Wales: An Intimate Portrait*. London, Little, Brown, 1994.

Heald, Tim, *The Duke: A Portrait of Prince Philip*. London, Hodder & Stoughton, 1991.

Hibbert, Christopher, *Queen Victoria: A Personal History*. London, HarperCollins, 2000.

Junor, Penny, *The Duchess: The Untold Story*. London, William Collins, 2017

Keay, Douglas, *Elizabeth II: Portrait of a Monarch*. London, Ebury Press, 1991.

Lacey, Robert, *Majesty: Queen Elizabeth II and the House of Windsor*. London, Sphere, 1977.

Marr, Andrew, *The Diamond Queen: Elizabeth II and Her People*. London, Macmillan, 2011.

McLeod, Kirsty, *Battle Royal: Edward VIII & George VI: Brother Against Brother*. London, Constable Robinson, 2000.

Morton, Andrew, *Diana: Her True Story*. London, Michael O'Mara, 1992.

Pimlott, Ben, *The Queen: A Biography of Elizabeth II*. Hoboken, NJ, John Wiley, 1997.

Rhodes, Margaret, *The Final Curtsey*. Edinburgh, Birlinn, 2012.

Shawcross, William, *Queen and Country*. London, BBC, 2002.

Smith, Sean, *Kate Unauthorised*. London, Simon & Schuster, 2012.

Vickers, Hugo, *Elizabeth, The Queen Mother*. London, Arrow, 2005.

Warwick, Christopher, *Princess Margaret: A Life of Contrasts*. London, Andre Deutsch, 2000.

Wilson, A. N., *The Rise and Fall of the House of Windsor*. London, Fawcett Books, 1994.

Ziegler, Philip, *King Edward VIII*. London, HarperCollins, 2012

Queen Elizabeth II and Prince Philip wave to the crowd along The Mall in London during a weekend of celebrations marking the Queen's 90th birthday and 63-year reign, June 12, 2016.

INDEX

Page numbers in italic denote an illustration